? ESSENTIAL QUESTIONS JOURNAL

PEARSON AMERICAN
GOVERNMENT

PEARSON

Boston, Massachusetts   Chandler, Arizona   Glenview, Illinois   Upper Saddle River, New Jersey

Pearson ® is a trademark, in the U.S. and/or in other countries, of Pearson plc or its affiliates.
Prentice Hall ® is a trademark, in the U.S. and/or in other countries, of Pearson Education, Inc., or its affiliates.

ISBN 10: 0-13-365674-8
ISBN 13: 978-0-13-365674-9
7 8 9 10   V016   13 12 11

Table of Contents

Table of Contents

How to Use This Book

The **Essential Questions Journal** will help you to better understand the principles of American government using questions and activities. Use this journal to develop the framework for your responses to the Essential Questions found in *Magruder's American Government* and *Foundations Series: American Government*. As you build your understanding and answer the Chapter Essential Questions, you will begin to shape your response to the overarching Unit Essential Questions.

The **Unit Essential Question** helps you to think about how fundamental principles of government shape your world.

The **Unit and Chapter Warmups** help you to begin thinking about the important ideas and Essential Questions of each unit and chapter. They tap into what you already know and set you on a path to learning more.

The **Chapter Essential Question** addresses the main idea of each chapter and contributes to the answer you are forming for the Unit Essential Question.

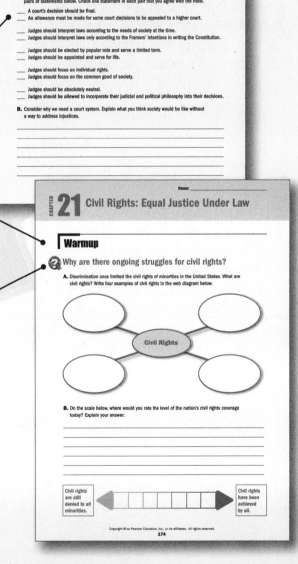

How to Use This Book

The engaging questions and activities in the **Chapter Explorations** challenge you to think creatively and use what you learn about the main ideas and political terms of the chapter. They also help you to form your responses to the Chapter and Unit Essential Questions.

→ Find Out activities direct you to discover, organize, and record knowledge that you will need to respond to the Essential Questions. You may review your print or online textbook or other sources, such as newspapers, news magazines, and the Internet, to help with your answers.

What Do You Think? activities ask you to synthesize information from Find Out items and your own prior knowledge to draw conclusions about various political issues and situations. These activities also guide you in exploring your opinions about government and examining supporting details and evidence from your own experiences and reading.

CHAPTER 21 Why are there ongoing struggles for civil rights? Name: _____

Exploration

I. Discrimination

→ Find Out

A. The Declaration of Independence declares that "all men are created equal," and the 14th Amendment guarantees "equal protection of the laws" to all Americans. Still, discrimination of minorities was the norm until civil rights acts were passed in the 1950s. In the chart below, use information in your print or online textbook to show the effects of discrimination.

Cause	Effect(s) on Minority Group
1. *Plessy* v. *Ferguson*, 1896, legalizes race-based discrimination.	
2. Westward expansion leads to the forced relocation of Native Americans to reservations.	
3. White Americans resent Chinese contract laborers who work in mines and on railroads.	
4. Japan bombs Pearl Harbor, bringing the United States into World War II.	
5. Women are placed in a separate "sphere" of society by men.	

What Do You Think?

B. In his "Letter From Birmingham Jail," civil rights leader Dr. Martin Luther King, Jr., wrote: "Oppressed people cannot remain oppressed forever. The yearning for freedom eventually manifests itself." In what ways did the struggle for civil rights manifest itself?

_____
_____
_____

The **Apply What You've Learned Activity** pages allow you to experience real-life perspectives on the chapter Essential Questions. The **Chapter Essay** page provides you with various perspectives related to the Chapter Essential Question. These pages will help you synthesize your ideas for responding to the Chapter Essential Question and for writing your Chapter Essay.

The **Apply What You've Learned Activity** worksheet helps you to complete the Apply What You've Learned Activity in your textbook. This activity will help you extend your thinking and draw conclusions about the Chapter Essential Question.

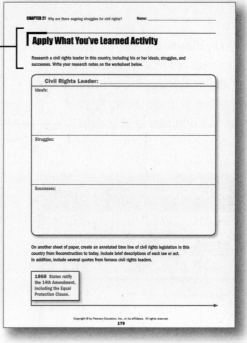

The **Chapter Essay** begins with quotations, facts, or images that relate to the Chapter Essential Question. The second part asks for your thoughts on this information, the Guiding Questions in your textbook, and the activities you have completed in your journal.

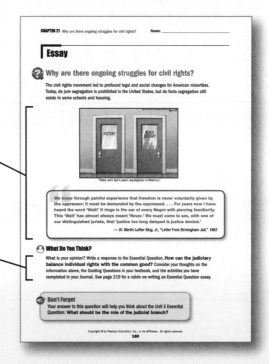

How to Use This Book

The **Unit Essay Warmup** and **Unit Essay** will help you focus your thinking on the Unit Essential Question. The Unit Essay Warmup asks questions about materials related to the main topics of the unit. The Unit Essay page also provides a graphic organizer to help you organize your thoughts about the Unit Essential Question. These pages also help you be better prepared for essay exams in school and standardized tests.

The **Unit Essay Warmup** gives you several different perspectives related to the main concept of the unit. The questions that follow each perspective help you to clarify your thoughts on the Unit Essential Question.

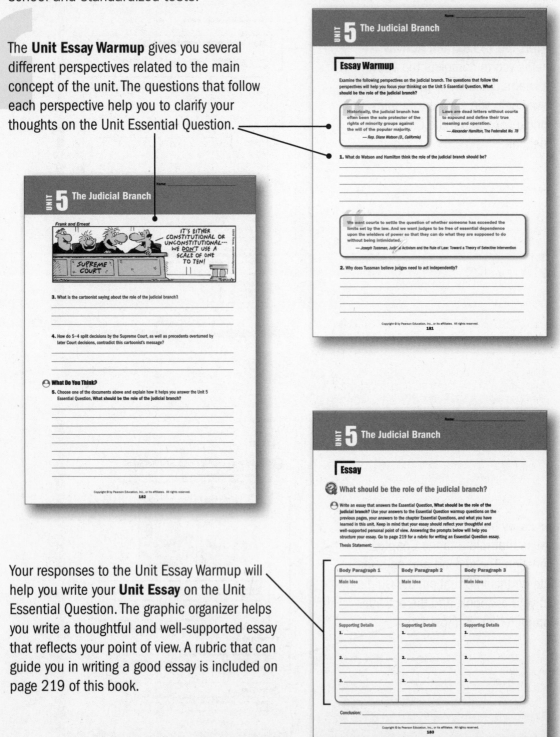

Your responses to the Unit Essay Warmup will help you write your **Unit Essay** on the Unit Essential Question. The graphic organizer helps you write a thoughtful and well-supported essay that reflects your point of view. A rubric that can guide you in writing a good essay is included on page 219 of this book.

Unit 1

Foundations of American Government

 Essential Question

What should be the goals of government?

Chapter 1 Essential Question

Is government necessary?

Chapter 2 Essential Question

How does the Constitution reflect the times in which it was written?

Chapter 3 Essential Question

How has the Constitution lasted through changing times?

Chapter 4 Essential Question

Is the federal system the best way to govern the United States?

UNIT 1 Foundations of American Government

Warmup

Philadelphia's Independence Hall was the birthplace of the Constitution of the United States.

What should be the goals of government?

Like cities, writing, art, and religion, government has always gone hand in hand with civilization. People do not seem to be able to live together without government. It regulates, organizes, and protects society. In Unit 1, you will study the goals and purposes of government and explore the possible answers to the Essential Question above.

A. Study the chart of specific activities that governments usually do. In your opinion, what are the three most important activities of government? Circle them.

Organize	Protect	Regulate
Maintain food supplies	Safeguard territory	Punish crimes
Provide for the needy	Defend the citizenry	Manage trade
Collect taxes	Build defenses	Manage public lands
Develop resources	Set up armies	Oversee trade/business
Establish public schools	Care for the environment	Police alcohol/drugs
Manage resources	Safeguard consumers	

B. What are three additional activities of government?

Organize: _____

Protect: _____

Regulate: _____

C. Are there any activities that you believe government should NEVER take part in? Explain your answer.

_____

_____

CHAPTER 1 **Principles of Government**

Warmup

 Is government necessary?

A. Read the quotation below from Alexander Hamilton, a statesman and an officer in the American Revolution.

> " Why has government been instituted at all? Because the passions of men will not conform to the dictates of reason and justice, without constraint.
>
> — *Alexander Hamilton,* The Federalist No. 11, *1787*

Do you agree or disagree with Hamilton? Explain your answer.

_____

_____

_____

_____

_____

_____

B. How important is government to your personal well-being? Use the scale to show your response. Explain your answer.

_____

_____

_____

_____

_____

_____

| Not Important | | | | | | | | | | Extremely Important |

Exploration

I. Government and the State

➔ Find Out

A. Every nation state has population, territory, sovereignty, and government. Give two examples of nation states. Identify the population, territory, and type of government of each one, using an almanac, encyclopedia, the Internet, or other sources. Identify the sources used.

1. Nation State: _____

Population: _____

Territory: _____

Type of Government: _____

Source(s): _____

_____

2. Nation State: _____

Population: _____

Territory: _____

Type of Government: _____

Source(s): _____

_____

B. Philosophers have long tried to explain the origin of the state. Over time, four major theories have evolved. Identify and define these theories, using your print or online textbook or other sources.

Theories of the Origin of the State
1.
2.
3.
4.

👤 What Do You Think?

C. Which theory of the origin of the state do you think makes the most sense? Explain.

_____

_____

_____

→ Find Out

D. Read the Preamble to the Constitution. Then list the six purposes of our government outlined there.

1. _____

_____

_____

2. _____

_____

_____

3. _____

_____

_____

4. _____

_____

_____

5. _____

_____

_____

6. _____

_____

_____

👤 What Do You Think?

E. Which purpose of government do you consider most important? Why?

_____

_____

_____

II. Forms of Government

→ Find Out

A. Review the forms of government in your print or online textbook to complete the chart below.

Form of Government	Example	Purposes
Democracy Unitary Federal Presidential Parliamentary		
Dictatorship Autocracy Oligarchy		

◉ What Do You Think?

B. How do the purposes of democracy and dictatorship differ? Explain your answer.

_____

_____

_____

_____

III. Basic Concepts of Democracy

➔ Find Out

A. Review the guiding principles of United States democracy in your print or online textbook. Then complete the chart below.

Definition of Basic Ideas	Significance: What Does It Mean?
Worth of the Individual	Example:
Equality of Every Person	Example:
Majority Rule, Minority Rights	Example:
Need for Compromise	Example:
Individual Freedom	Example:

👤 What Do You Think?

B. Responsibilities of a good citizen include voting (starting at age 18), staying informed, and volunteering. Should these responsibilities become duties, required by law? Explain.

_____

_____

_____

➡️ Find Out

C. The economic system of a state is different from its government. However, all modern states have a role in overseeing or regulating the economy. What are the most important features of the U.S. economy? Review these features in your print or online textbook or other sources. Then complete the Venn diagram below.

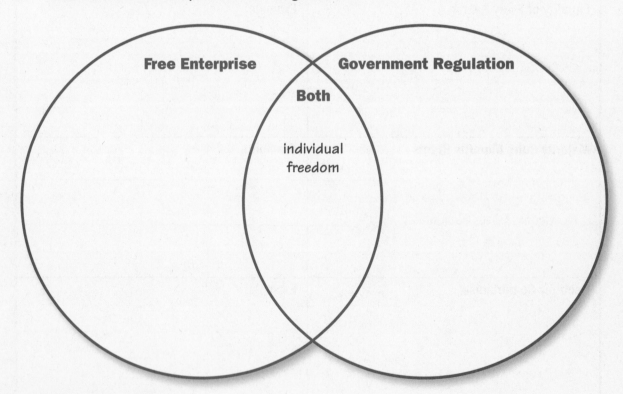

Free Enterprise

Government Regulation

Both

individual freedom

👤 What Do You Think?

D. How much should your government oversee the economy? Explain your answer.

_____

_____

_____

Apply What You've Learned Activity

Suppose that you were to create a government for a country formed from previously independent states. Use this worksheet to help you complete the Apply What You've Learned questions in your print or online textbook.

A. Check each classification that applies to this government.

1. ☐ Democracy ☐ Dictatorship

2. ☐ Unitary ☐ Federal ☐ Confederate

3. ☐ Presidential ☐ Parliamentary

B. Can all citizens participate in this government? Explain. _____

_____

_____

_____

_____

C. Are the legislative and executive branches separate and independent? _____

_____

D. What powers does each branch hold? _____

_____

_____

_____

_____

E. Does the new nation run under a free enterprise system? _____

_____

F. How much power does the government have to oversee the economy? _____

_____

_____

_____

Essay

 ## Is government necessary?

Political thinkers, philosophers, and historians have all had their say about government. Humorists have also weighed in on this topic. Each quotation below has an amusing approach to a serious message.

> **The worst thing in this world, next to anarchy, is government.**
>
> — *Henry Ward Beecher,* Proverbs from Plymouth Pulpit, *1887*

> **If government were a product, selling it would be illegal.**
>
> — *P. J. O'Rourke,* The Liberty Manifesto

What Do You Think?

What is your opinion? Write a response to the Essential Question, **Is government necessary?** Consider your thoughts on the quotations above, the Guiding Questions in your textbook, and the activities you have done in your Journal. See page 219 for a rubric on writing an Essential Question essay.

 Don't Forget

Your answer to this question will help you think about the Unit 1 Essential Question: **What should be the goals of government?**

Origins of American Government

Warmup

How does the Constitution reflect the times in which it was written?

A. What do you know about the times in which the Constitution was written? Write **T** (True), **F** (False), or **NS** (Not sure) for each statement below.

1. _____ Each of the thirteen colonies had its own legislature that enacted laws.

2. _____ In the mid-1700s, Great Britain's parliament took little part in the local affairs of the colonies.

3. _____ In the 1760s, Great Britain's harsh tax and trade policies fanned colonial resentment.

4. _____ The Declaration of Independence outlined the colonial grievances against Great Britain.

5. _____ The colonies adopted constitutions after the Declaration of Independence was signed.

6. _____ The Articles of Confederation set up the first National Government after independence.

7. _____ Government under the Articles of Confederation had no executive or judiciary branches.

8. _____ The Articles of Confederation gave the Congress no power to tax.

9. _____ Slavery was an important issue at the Constitutional Convention of 1787.

10. _____ All Framers were satisfied with the compromises that resulted in the new Constitution.

CHAPTER 2 How does the Constitution reflect the times in which it was written?

Name: _____

Exploration

I. Our Political Beginnings

➔ Find Out

A. The colonies have been called "the 13 schools of government." Identify which colonies fall into each type, and describe their government, using your print or online textbook or other sources.

Type of Colony	Government
Royal colonies, as of 1775 1. New Hampshire 2. 3. 4. 5. 6. 7. 8.	**Governor:** named by the king to serve as colony's chief executive **Legislature:** bicameral; upper house, a council, named by the king; lower house elected by property owners qualified to vote; laws had to be approved by governor and crown
Proprietary colonies, as of 1775 1. 2. 3.	**Governor:** **Legislature:**
Charter colonies, as of 1775 1. 2.	**Governor:** **Legislature:**

CHAPTER 2 How does the Constitution reflect the times in which it was written?

Name: _____

👤 What Do You Think?

B. Some historians believe that if Britain had given all the colonies the freedoms that were given to the Charter colonies, the American Revolution might never have occurred. Why do you think they argue this point?

_____

_____

_____

_____

II. The Coming of Independence

➔ Find Out

A. Read the Declaration of Independence. Then make a list of the four most important colonial grievances against King George III. Number them in order of importance.

1. _____

_____ Number _____

2. _____

_____ Number _____

3. _____

_____ Number _____

4. _____

_____ Number _____

👤 What Do You Think?

B. Explain your ranking.

_____

_____

_____

_____

➔ Find Out

C. States drafted constitutions after the Declaration of Independence. On a separate sheet of paper, name four common features and explain the importance of each one.

CHAPTER 2 How does the Constitution reflect the times in which it was written?

Name: _____

III. The Critical Period

➔ Find Out

A. Use your print or online textbook or other sources to help you identify the main weaknesses of the Articles of Confederation.

Weaknesses of the Articles of Confederation
1.
2.
3.
4.
5.
6.

👤 What Do You Think?

B. What were some effects of these weaknesses?

_____

_____

_____

_____

_____

C. Which weaknesses do you think were most important to the Framers as they began drafting a new constitution? Explain your response.

_____

_____

_____

_____

_____

CHAPTER 2 How does the Constitution reflect the times in which it was written?

Name: _____

Find Out

D. Use your print or online textbook or other sources to help you identify two Enlightenment philosophers who influenced the Founders of our nation and the Framers of our Constitution. Then fill in a fact card for each.

Philosopher: _____	Philosopher: _____
Date of birth/death: _____	Date of birth/death: _____
Country of birth: _____	Country of birth: _____
Important work: _____	Important work: _____
_____	_____
Important ideas: _____	Important ideas: _____
_____	_____
_____	_____
Influence: _____	Influence: _____
_____	_____
_____	_____

IV. Creating the Constitution

Find Out

A. Review the Virginia and New Jersey Plans offered at the Constitutional Convention of 1787. Then complete the Venn diagram below.

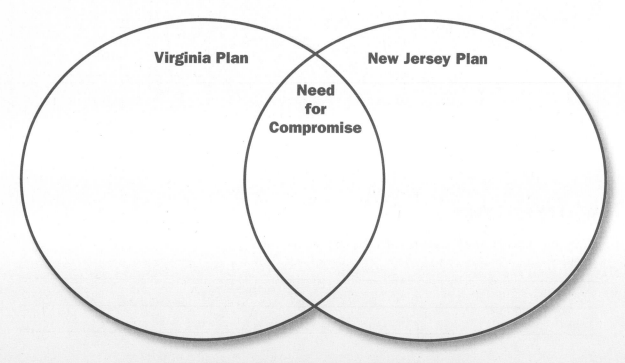

Virginia Plan

Need for Compromise

New Jersey Plan

CHAPTER 2 How does the Constitution reflect the times in which it was written?

Name: _____

What Do You Think?

B. The Connecticut Compromise has been called "The Great Compromise," while the Three-Fifths Compromise has been called "The Sectional Compromise." Do you think these are appropriate terms? Why or why not?

_____
_____
_____
_____

V. Ratifying the Constitution

Find Out

A. After the Constitutional Convention, two groups emerged—those opposing and those favoring ratification. Use your print or online textbook, or other sources, to identify their positions on each issue and the reasons that supported each view.

Issue	Federalists	Anti-Federalists
Increased power of central government		
Lack of a bill of rights		
A powerful executive branch		
Ratification process		
Absence of mention of God		
Other issue:		

What Do You Think?

B. In your opinion, which issue is most relevant today? Why?

_____
_____

CHAPTER 2 How does the Constitution reflect the times in which it was written?

Name: _____

Apply What You've Learned Activity

Research a national constitution that has been created in recent years. Use this worksheet to answer the Apply What You've Learned questions in your print or online textbook.

A. The list below contains examples of countries with a new constitution. Circle a country to research or find another.

Armenia **(2005)**   Kosovo **(2008)**

Afghanistan **(2004)**   Qatar **(2005)**

Myanmar [Burma] **(2008)**   Sudan **(2005)**

Gibraltar **(2007)**   Swaziland **(2006)**

Iraq **(2005)**   Thailand **(2007)**

B. Who wrote the constitution? What were the qualifications of the writer(s)?

_____

_____

_____

C. What steps did the writer(s) use to write the constitution?

_____

_____

_____

_____

D. What rights does the constitution protect?

_____

_____

_____

E. What was the ratification process?

_____

_____

_____

_____

CHAPTER 2 How does the Constitution reflect the times in which it was written?

Name: _____

Essay

How does the Constitution reflect the times in which it was written?

Return to the Warmup Activity on page 11, and review the list of statements for which you responded True, False, or Not Sure. Then answer the questions below.

A. Which statements would you answer differently now?

_____

_____

B. Which statements are most helpful in understanding the Chapter Essential Question?

_____

_____

_____

C. Explain your thinking on question B above.

_____

_____

_____

What Do You Think?

What is your opinion? Write a response to the Essential Question, **How does the Constitution reflect the times in which it was written?** Consider your thoughts on the questions above, the Guiding Questions in your textbook, and the activities you have done in your Journal. See page 219 for a rubric on writing an Essential Question essay.

Don't Forget
Your answer to this question will help you think about the Unit 1 Essential Question: **What should be the goals of government?**

CHAPTER 3 The Constitution

Warmup

 How has the Constitution lasted through changing times?

Study the "Then and Now" chart, below, that shows important changes in the United States since the Constitution was ratified in 1788.

Then and Now	1790	2008
Number of states	13	50
Population	3,893,635 (includes ME, VT, KY)	303,834,636
Number of Slaves	694,280 (includes ME, VT, KY)	0
Right to Vote	White male property owners	All citizens regardless of gender, race, religion, or ethnic background
Budget Deficit	75 million dollars	407 billion dollars
Average Life Expectancy	19–25 years	77.2 years
Economy	Agricultural/rural	Corporate/service/urban

What does the chart suggest about the Constitution's durability?

_____

_____

_____

_____

_____

CHAPTER 3 How has the Constitution lasted through changing times?

Name: _____

Exploration

I. The Six Basic Principles

Find Out

A. How have the six basic principles contributed to the long life of the Constitution? Define each principle, using your print or online textbook or other sources. Then explain the importance of each one to the Constitution's longevity.

Definition	Importance to the Constitution's Longevity
1. Popular Sovereignty Political power resides in the people.	Because citizens can vote and have a say in their government, they are more willing to work and compromise for the common good.
2. Limited Government	
3. Separation of Powers	
4. Checks and Balances	
5. Judicial Review	
6. Federalism	

CHAPTER 3 How has the Constitution lasted through changing times?

Name: _____

II. Formal Amendment

➡ Find Out

A. Of the 27 constitutional amendments, 26 were adopted in the same manner. Describe this method of amendment.

_____
_____
_____

👤 What Do You Think?

B. Why do you think this method has been used most often?

_____
_____
_____

➡ Find Out

C. Use your print or online textbook, the Constitution, or other sources to identify the subject of each amendment below.

1. 19th Amendment
Subject: _____

2. 24th Amendment
Subject: _____

3. 26th Amendment
Subject: _____

4. 22nd Amendment
Subject: _____

5. 13th Amendment
Subject: _____

6. 1st Amendment
Subject: _____

👤 What Do You Think?

D. Which amendment has the greatest effect on your life? Why?

_____
_____

Name: _____

III. Change by Other Means

➔ Find Out

A. Identify the five major agents of change in our government, using your print or online textbook or other sources. Then give two examples of change for each one.

Agent of Change	Examples of Change
1. Congress	Example 1: Set up federal courts (except Supreme Court) Example 2:
2.	Example 1: Example 2:
3.	Example 1: Example 2:
4.	Example 1: Example 2:
5.	Example 1: Example 2:

👤 What Do You Think?

B. Have these five agents of change contributed to the long life of the Constitution? Explain your answer.

_____

_____

_____

Name: _____

Apply What You've Learned Activity

Congress has proposed over 10,000 joint resolutions calling for constitutional amendments. The list of failed amendments may suggest an idea for the amendment proposal that you will create for the Apply What You've Learned Activity. Use the table below to summarize arguments for and against your subject for amendment.

Subject for Amendment:

_____

Arguments in favor	
	_____
	_____
	_____
	_____
	_____
	_____
Arguments opposed	_____
	_____
	_____
	_____
	_____
	_____

A. Which three arguments in favor of the amendment do you think are strongest?

_____

_____

_____

B. How would you answer the three strongest arguments opposed to the amendment?

_____

_____

_____

_____

CHAPTER 3 How has the Constitution lasted through changing times?

Name: _____

Essay

How has the Constitution lasted through changing times?

The United States Constitution is one of the oldest written constitutions in the world. This chapter should help you to understand the longevity of what British prime minister William Gladstone called, "the most wonderful work ever struck off at a given time by the brain and purpose of man." Read the following quotations about the Constitution.

> The United States Constitution has proved itself the most marvelously elastic compilation of rules of government ever written.
>
> — *Franklin D. Roosevelt, 32nd President*

> The Constitution of the United States was made not merely for the generation that then existed, but for posterity—unlimited, undefined, endless, perpetual posterity.
>
> — *Henry Clay, Senator and Statesman, Speech in the Senate, January 29, 1850*

> It is the genius of our Constitution that under its shelter of enduring institutions and rooted principles there is ample room for the rich fertility of American political invention.
>
> — *Lyndon B. Johnson, 36th President*

What Do You Think?

What is your opinion? Write a response to the Essential Question, **How has the Constitution lasted through changing times?** Consider your thoughts on the quotations above, the Guiding Questions in your textbook, and the activities you have done in your Journal. See page 219 for a rubric on writing an Essential Question essay.

Don't Forget

Your answer to this question will help you think about the Unit 1 Essential Question: **What should be the goals of government?**

Name: _____

Warmup

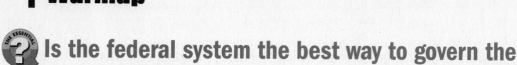 **Is the federal system the best way to govern the United States?**

A. The words *E Pluribus Unum* first appeared on U.S. coins in 1795. The Latin phrase also appears on the Great Seal of the United States. Its translation is "out of many, one." What is the meaning of this motto for our nation?

_____

_____

_____

B. Picture the flag of the United States. What is the symbolism of the 50 stars together on the ocean-blue rectangle?

_____

_____

_____

C. Given what you know about how the U.S. government runs, do you think this symbolism is fitting? Explain.

_____

_____

_____

D. Which of the following images best reflects the relationship between the State governments and the National Government: a ship and its sails; a building and its columns; a tree and its branches? Explain your answer.

_____

_____

_____

_____

CHAPTER 4 Is the federal system the best way to govern the
United States?

Name: _____

Exploration

I. The Powers of Congress

→ Find Out

A. Read Article 1, Section 8 of the U.S. Constitution. Then list the most important expressed
powers of Congress.

1. _____
2. _____
3. _____
4. _____
5. _____
6. _____
7. _____
8. _____
9. _____
10. _____

B. Use your print or online textbook or other sources to review the national, State, and
concurrent powers. Then complete the Venn diagram below.

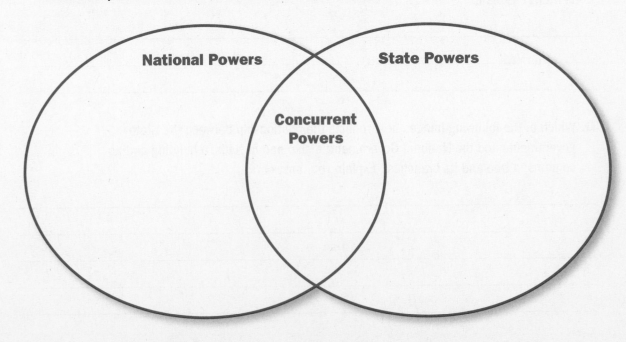

National Powers

State Powers

Concurrent
Powers

Name: _____

II. The National Government and the Fifty States

→ Find Out

A. What are the three most basic obligations of the National Government to the States? Use your print or online textbook or other sources to identify and define each one.

1. _____

2. _____

3. _____

👤 What Do You Think?

B. How do the obligations of the National Government help to protect the federal system?

_____

_____

_____

→ Find Out

C. Review the three following areas of inter-governmental cooperation. Then define and give an example of each one.

1. Federal Grants-in-Aid

Definition: _____

Example: _____

2. Revenue Sharing

Definition: _____

Example: _____

3. State Aid to National Government

Definition: _____

Example: _____

👤 What Do You Think?

D. How do these financial arrangements help to protect the federal system?

_____

_____

_____

CHAPTER 4 Is the federal system the best way to govern the
United States?

Name: _____

III. Interstate Relations

➡ Find Out

A. Several provisions of the Constitution deal with the States' relationships with one
another. Use your print or online textbook or other sources to help you define the
following provisions and give an example of each one. Then explain how each provision
helps to protect the federal system.

Interstate Compacts Definition: Example:	**Protects the federal system by:**
Full Faith and Credit Definition: Example:	**Protects the federal system by:**
Extradition Definition: Example:	**Protects the federal system by:**
Privileges and Immunities Definition: Example:	**Protects the federal system by:**

👤 What Do You Think?

B. Which provision is most important in preventing conflict among the States? Why?

_____

_____

_____

CHAPTER 4 Is the federal system the best way to govern the United States?

Name: _____

Apply What You've Learned Activity

How could your community benefit from a federal grant? Use the table below to summarize the results of your research for your proposed community grant from the Federal Government, as outlined in the Apply What You've Learned questions in your print or online textbook.

What type of grant is most needed in your community and why? ☐ Block ☐ Categorical ☐ Project	_____ _____ _____ _____ _____
What kinds of agencies, departments, and/or organizations would benefit from the grant you selected?	_____ _____ _____ _____
How much money is available from this grant?	_____ _____ _____ _____
What requirements are there for receiving this grant?	_____ _____ _____ _____

A. What kind of conditions might be attached to your grant?

_____

_____

_____

B. How did you determine which part of your community would benefit most?

_____

_____

_____

CHAPTER 4 Is the federal system the best way to govern the United States?

Name: _____

Essay

Is the federal system the best way to govern the United States?

As you read the quotations about federalism below, keep in mind the weaknesses of the Articles of Confederation. Also remember why the States feared a strong Federal Government after the Revolution.

> This balance between the National and State governments ought to be dwelt on with peculiar attention, as it is of the utmost importance. It forms a double security to the people. If one encroaches on their rights they will find a powerful protection in the other.
>
> — *Alexander Hamilton, 1788 Speech to the New York Ratifying Convention*

> The operations of the federal government will be most extensive and important in times of war and danger; those of the State governments, in times of peace and security.
>
> — *James Madison,* Federalist No. 45, *1788*

What Do You Think?

What is your opinion? Write a response to the Essential Question, **Is the federal system the best way to govern the United States?** Consider your thoughts on the quotations above, the Guiding Questions in your textbook, and the activities you have done in your Journal. See page 219 for a rubric on writing an Essential Question essay.

Don't Forget

Your answer to this question will help you think about the Unit 1 Essential Question: **What should be the goals of government?**

UNIT 1 Foundations of American Government

Essay Warmup

Examine the following perspectives on the goals of government. The questions that follow each perspective will help you focus your thinking on the Unit 1 Essential Question, **What should be the goals of government?**

> **A wise and frugal [thrifty] government . . . shall restrain men from injuring one another, shall leave them otherwise free to regulate their own pursuits of industry and improvement, and shall not take from the mouth of labor the bread it has earned. This is the sum of good government.**
>
> — *Thomas Jefferson,* First Inaugural Address, *March 4, 1801*

1. According to Thomas Jefferson, what are three goals of government?

■ _____

_____

■ _____

_____

■ _____

_____

2. Which of these goals do you think is most important? Why?

_____

_____

_____

_____

3. Would you add any goals to Jefferson's list? Why or why not?

_____

_____

_____

_____

Reproduced by permission of Johnny Hart and Field Enterprises

4. What point is the cartoonist making about government?

_____

_____

_____

> **Good government is a trust, and the officers of the government are trustees; and both the trust and the trustees are created for the benefit of the people.**
>
> *— Henry Clay, Speech at Ashland, Kentucky, 1829*

5. Is Clay's quotation or the cartoon closer to your perspective on government? Explain.

_____

_____

_____

🙂 What Do You Think?

6. Choose one of the documents above and explain how it helps you answer the Unit 1 Essential Question, **What should be the goals of government?**

_____

_____

_____

_____

_____

UNIT 1 Foundations of American Government

Essay

What should be the goals of government?

Write an essay that answers the Unit 1 Essential Question, **What should be the goals of government?** Use your answers to the Essential Question warmup questions on the previous pages, your answers to the chapter Essential Questions, and what you have learned in this unit. Keep in mind that your essay should reflect your thoughtful and well-supported personal point of view. Answering the prompts below will help you structure your essay. Go to page 219 for a rubric for writing an Essential Question essay.

Thesis Statement: _____

_____

Body Paragraph 1	Body Paragraph 2	Body Paragraph 3
Main Idea _____ _____ _____ _____	**Main Idea** _____ _____ _____ _____	**Main Idea** _____ _____ _____ _____
Supporting Details 1. _____ _____ _____ 2. _____ _____ _____ 3. _____ _____	**Supporting Details** 1. _____ _____ _____ 2. _____ _____ _____ 3. _____ _____	**Supporting Details** 1. _____ _____ _____ 2. _____ _____ _____ 3. _____ _____

Conclusion: _____

_____

Political Behavior: Government by the People

Essential Question

In what ways should people participate in public affairs?

Chapter 5
Essential Question

Does the two-party system help or harm democracy?

Chapter 6
Essential Question

Why do voters act as they do?

Chapter 7
Essential Question

How fair and effective is the electoral process?

Chapter 8
Essential Question

What is the place of the media and public opinion in a democracy?

Chapter 9
Essential Question

To what extent do interest groups advance or harm democracy?

UNIT 2 Political Behavior: Government by the People

Warmup

In what ways should people participate in public affairs?

Our system of government guarantees its citizens many rights. It also places upon them many responsibilities. In Unit 2, you will explore the various ways in which citizens can and do take part in public affairs as you build an answer to the Essential Question above.

For American citizens, voting is both a right and a responsibility.

A. Think about the term *public affairs* in the Essential Question above. What do you think this term means? Include examples to help illustrate your answer.

_____

_____

_____

_____

_____

_____

_____

B. Review your answer above. Based on your understanding of the term *public affairs,* create a list of the five most important responsibilities a citizen has for taking part in public affairs.

1. _____

2. _____

3. _____

4. _____

5. _____

CHAPTER **5** **Political Parties**

Warmup

 Does the two-party system help or harm democracy?

A. When you think of the term *political party*, what comes to mind? What do you think political parties do in our system? What associations do you make with this term? In the chart below, record some positive associations, or impressions, you hold about political parties and some negative associations.

Political Parties	
Positive Associations	**Negative Associations**
•	•
•	•
•	•

B. Think about what you know about how political parties work in our system of government, and then answer the questions below.

1. What are some possible advantages of having only two powerful political parties?

_____

_____

2. What are some possible disadvantages of having only two powerful political parties?

_____

_____

Exploration

I. What Political Parties Do

➡ **Find Out**

A. A political party is a complicated concept. It includes a number of different parts and components. Using your print or online textbook, identify and describe the elements that answer the question, "What is a party?"

1. _____

_____

2. _____

_____

3. _____

_____

B. Using your print or online textbook, identify five different roles filled by political parties in our system of government, and record them in the concept web below. Include an example or explanation of each role in the balloon.

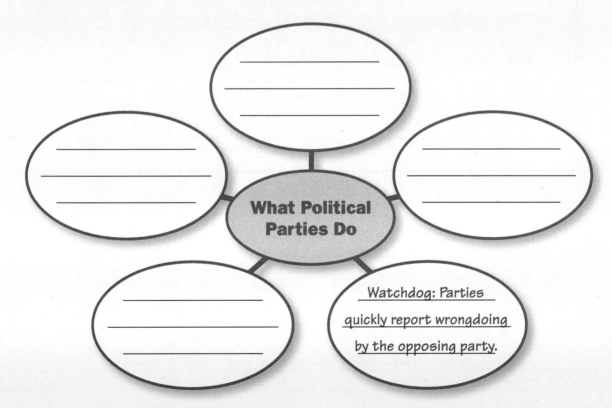

What Do You Think?

C. The Framers were generally not in favor of political parties, and the Constitution does not include any mention of them. Yet parties quickly appeared in the new nation. What might government be like if there were no political parties? Could government as we know it function without them? Why or why not?

_____

_____

_____

_____

II. Why Do We Have a Two-Party System?

Find Out

A. Review the history of the development of political parties in the United States. Then record details of the significance of each of the events listed in the chart below as they relate to the rise of political parties.

Development of Political Parties			
Ratification Debate	Conflicts During Washington's Presidency	Adams's Presidency	Election of 1800

B. Using your print or online textbook, identify four different reasons for the development of our two-party system.

1. _____

_____

2. _____

_____

3. _____

_____

4. _____

_____

👤 What Do You Think?

C. What do you think are the strongest factors working to preserve the two-party system today? Explain your choices.

_____

_____

_____

_____

III. Alternatives to the Two-Party System

➜ Find Out

A. Review the structure of the parliamentary system of government. Compare and contrast that system of government with the two-party system by completing the Venn diagram, below.

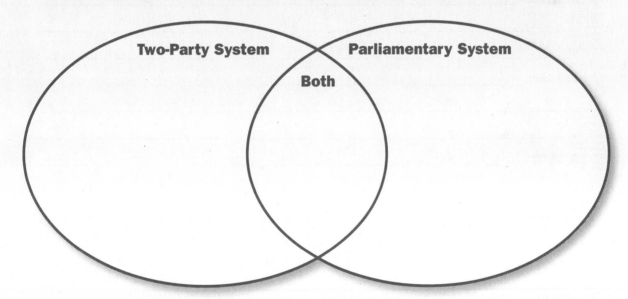

👤 What Do You Think?

B. Both multiparty systems and two-party systems are designed to be responsive to the people. That is, they are designed to promote the election of officials who represent and respond to the desires of voters. In your opinion, which system is most likely to be most responsive to voters? Explain.

_____

_____

_____

_____

→ Find Out

C. Using your print or online textbook or other sources, briefly describe the impact of minor political parties in the following presidential elections:

1. 1892: _____

_____

_____

2. 1912: _____

_____

_____

3. 1948: _____

_____

_____

4. 1968: _____

_____

_____

_____

5. 1992: _____

_____

_____

6. 2000: _____

_____

_____

👤 What Do You Think?

D. Why do you think it might be worth supporting a minor political party in the United States even if that candidate has little chance of winning?

_____

_____

_____

_____

_____

_____

_____

Apply What You've Learned Activity

In today's world, does it really matter to what party a person belongs? Use this worksheet to help you answer the Apply What You've Learned questions in your print or online textbook. Use the space below to record information about the party identification of the person you interview.

With what party does your subject identify?

_____

On what issues does your subject most closely agree and disagree with his or her party?

_____

_____

What might cause your subject to switch parties?

_____

_____

Does your subject think the two-party system helps or harms democracy?

_____

_____

A. Does your interview subject closely identify with a party?

_____

_____

B. Do you think your interview subject is likely to support the same party in a future election? Explain your answer.

_____

_____

C. Do you think your interview subject is more interested in the success of a particular party at the ballot box or in seeing certain policies enacted? Explain your answer.

_____

_____

Essay

Does the two-party system help or harm democracy?

Our system of government was designed to be democratic. However, it was not designed to have political parties—or the two-party system that has developed over time. As you read the quotations below, consider how, or if, the two-party system serves the needs and interests of the country.

> That's the real beauty of our two-party system. Neither major party is strong enough to win with just its stalwarts. The winner must capture a majority of independents, crossovers or newly registered voters.
>
> — USA Today *editorial, 2000*

> With a number of viable parties to choose from rather than only two, people tend to feel that their party truly embodies their specific interests, and hence they are more likely to vote.
>
> — *Martin P. Wattenberg,* The Boston Globe, *September 21, 2003*

What Do You Think?

What is your opinion? Write a response to the Essential Question, **Does the two-party system help or harm democracy?** Consider your thoughts on the quotations above, the Guiding Questions in your textbook, and the activities you have completed in your Journal. See page 219 for a rubric for writing an Essential Question essay.

Don't Forget

Your answer to this question will help you think about the Unit 2 Essential Question: **In what ways should people participate in public affairs?**

CHAPTER 6 Voters and Voter Behavior

Warmup

Why do voters act as they do?

A. Think about all the steps that might be involved with casting a ballot in an election. What steps must a voter take in order to carry out this task responsibly? Identify as many steps as you can and place them in the flowchart below.

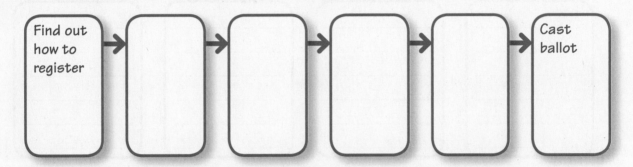

B. What are some of the factors that might prevent a person from casting a vote in an election?

1. _____
2. _____
3. _____
4. _____
5. _____
6. _____

C. Voting in an election requires that the voter choose between one of two or more candidates. What factors influence how a person votes in an election? List as many factors as you can think of here.

1. _____
2. _____
3. _____
4. _____
5. _____
6. _____

Exploration

I. The Right to Vote

➡ Find Out

A. When the United States came into being, voting rights were basically limited to white men who owned property. Using your print or online textbook or other sources, identify key developments in the expansion of voting rights. Record these events in the space provided, then connect them to the blank time line below.

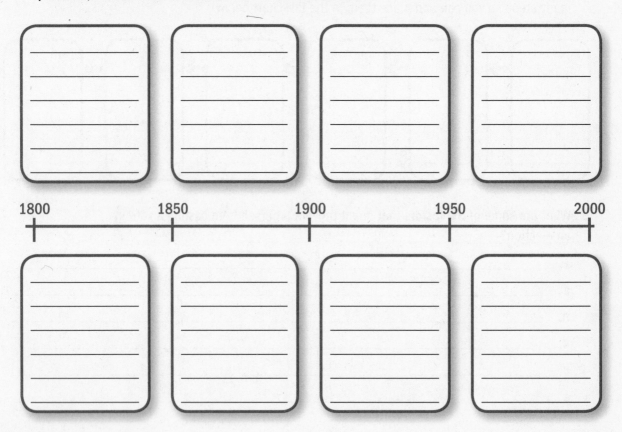

👤 What Do You Think?

B. Based on the information above, how would you describe the general attitude about voting rights and how it has changed over the history of the United States?

_____

_____

_____

_____

_____

👤 What Do You Think?

C. Why do you think the nation has expanded voting rights? What does this suggest about the importance of voting rights in the American system of government?

_____

_____

_____

II. Voter Qualifications

➡ Find Out

A. Using your print or online textbook or other sources, identify the requirements that a person wishing to vote today may have to meet. Also list the reasons that an otherwise eligible voter may be disqualified.

Possible Voter Qualifications	Possible Reasons for Voter Disqualification
•	•
•	•
•	•
•	•
•	•

B. Using your print or online textbook or other sources, identify the common concerns about voter registration in the United States, and what has been done in recent years to address those concerns.

Cause	Effect
Some people do not support voter registration because	The Federal Government responded to concerns by

⊙ Find Out

C. Another voting-related controversy in the United States is a move by some States to require identification for voting. Use your print or online textbook or other sources to learn about voter ID. Then summarize the two sides of the issue below:

For Voter ID   **Against Voter ID**

_____   _____

_____   _____

_____   _____

_____   _____

⊙ What Do You Think?

D. Based on what you have recorded above, what is the balance that the federal and State governments must strike when trying to establish voting requirements for the electorate?

_____

_____

_____

III. The Struggle for Civil Rights

⊙ Find Out

A. Using your print or online textbook or other sources, fill in the chart below with information about the long struggle for African American voting rights.

Cause
15th Amendment—African American men win voting rights

Effect
Some States responded by . . .
_____
_____
_____
_____
_____
_____
Cause

Effect
African Americans and others respond by . . .
_____
_____
_____
_____
_____
Cause

Effects
•
•
•
•

Name: _____

What Do You Think?

B. In the larger sense, the long struggle for civil rights was about human dignity and freedom. But more specifically, it was about voting rights. On a separate sheet of paper, write a paragraph that explains what this episode in United States history suggests about the importance of voting rights. Then address the following question: Despite the long and difficult struggle for voting rights, why do some people choose not to vote?

IV. Voter Behavior

Find Out

A. Use your print or online textbook or other sources to find data about voter turnout in the past four national elections. Use the information you have found to complete the circle graphs below.

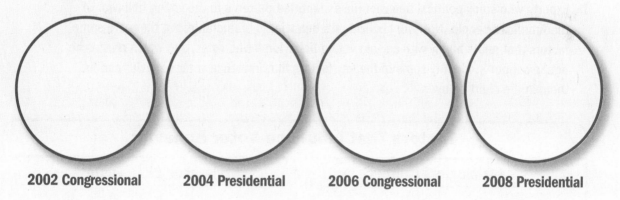

2002 Congressional   2004 Presidential   2006 Congressional   2008 Presidential

B. Voter turnout is low in the United States compared to many other democratic nations. Use your print or online textbook or other sources to find some possible reasons why millions of people do not take part in elections. List the possible reasons below.

■ _____

_____

■ _____

_____

■ _____

_____

■ _____

_____

■ _____

_____

Name: _____

What Do You Think?

C. Suppose you were talking to an eligible voter who was planning not to take part in an upcoming election. Make an argument in favor of taking part in elections that addresses some of the possible reasons for not voting.

_____

_____

_____

_____

_____

Find Out

D. Experts who study political behavior have identified patterns in the voting behavior of the American people. Not every individual's behavior is predictable, but there are some factors that relate highly with certain voting behaviors—who votes, and which parties he or she supports. Identify some of the key factors that influence voter behavior and list them in the chart below.

Factors That Influence Voter Behavior	
Sociological Factors	**Psychological Factors**
•	•
•	•
•	•
•	•
•	•
•	•

What Do You Think?

E. Suppose you were preparing to vote in an upcoming election. What are the issues and factors that you would consider in deciding your vote? Which factors seem unimportant? Write a brief summary of your decision-making process.

_____

_____

_____

Apply What You've Learned Activity

Use this worksheet to answer the Apply What You've Learned questions in your print or online textbook, and interview a voting-age adult in your community. Use the space below to summarize the information you collect.

Part I—Qualifying to Vote

Registration requirements

■ Where _____

■ When _____

Residency requirements

_____

Identification requirements

_____

Basis for voter disqualification

■ Mental competence standard: _____

■ Rules if dishonorably discharged from military: _____

■ Rules for voting for felons: _____

Where do you vote in your community? _____

Part II—Voter Attitudes

(a) _____

(b) _____

(c) _____

A. Did your interview subject know correctly how to register to vote in your community? Explain.

_____

_____

B. Do you agree with your subject's suggestions for improving voting procedures? Explain.

_____

_____

C. Do you think that the process for voting should be made easier or more difficult, or should it be left the same? Explain your answer.

_____

_____

Essay

Why do voters act as they do?

Few things are so closely linked to our understanding of democracy than the act of voting. The effort to secure and expand voting rights has been at the heart of some of this nation's fiercest struggles. As you read the quotations below, think about the meaning of the franchise to the American people.

> So long as I do not firmly and irrevocably possess the right to vote I do not possess myself. I cannot make up my mind—it is made up for me. I cannot live as a democratic citizen, observing the laws I have helped to enact—I can only submit to the edict of others.
>
> — *Martin Luther King, Jr.,* Give Us the Ballot, We Will Transform the South, *May 17, 1957*

> Under every view of the subject, it seems indispensable that the mass of the citizens should not be without a voice in making the laws which they are to obey, and in choosing the magistrates who are to administer them.
>
> — *James Madison at the Constitutional Convention, 1787*

What Do You Think?

What is your opinion? Write a response to the Essential Question, **Why do voters act as they do?** Consider your thoughts on the quotations above, the Guiding Questions in your textbook, and the activities you have completed in your Journal. See page 219 for a rubric for writing an Essential Question essay.

Don't Forget

Your answer to this question will help you think about the Unit 2 Essential Question: **In what ways should people participate in public affairs?**

CHAPTER

7 The Electoral Process

Warmup

 How fair and effective is the electoral process?

A. Think about the words *fair* and *effective*. On the lines below, write down some words or phrases that you think are necessary to produce a fair and effective electoral process.

To be fair, the electoral process must

- _____
- _____
- _____
- _____

To be effective, the electoral process must

- _____
- _____
- _____
- _____

B. Using the criteria you identified above, and based on your impressions of the electoral process in the United States, rate the process on a scale of one to ten (with one being the lowest rating and ten being the highest). Briefly explain the reasons for your rating on the lines provided.

1   2   3   4   5   6   7   8   9   10

Reason _____

_____

_____

1   2   3   4   5   6   7   8   9   10

Reason _____

_____

_____

Exploration

I. The Nomination Process

→ Find Out

A. Nomination is the process of formally naming candidates to appear on the ballot in an election. It is the first step in the election process, and it is often performed by a political party. Using your print or online textbook or other sources, identify and describe the major methods by which nomination occurs in our system.

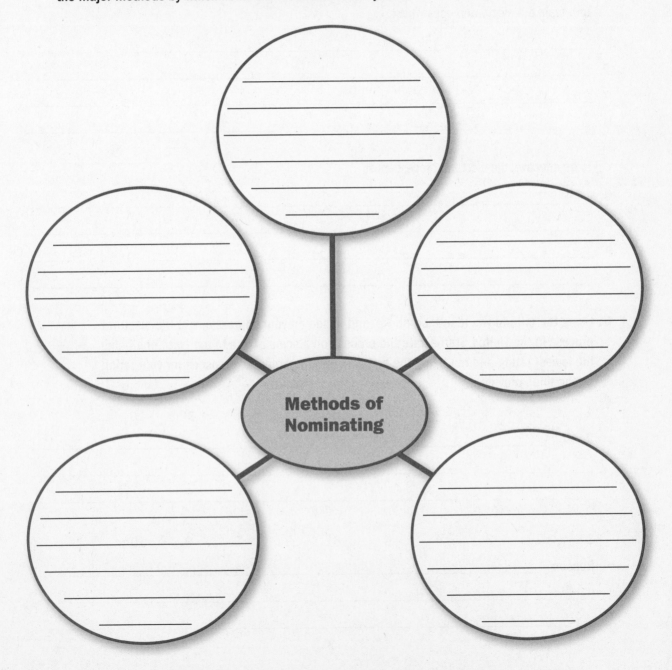

Methods of Nominating

B. Today, the direct primary is used to nominate candidates to many high-level offices. Use your print or online textbook or other sources to learn about the different types of primaries. Then use what you have learned to compare and contrast the different types of primaries in the Venn diagram, below.

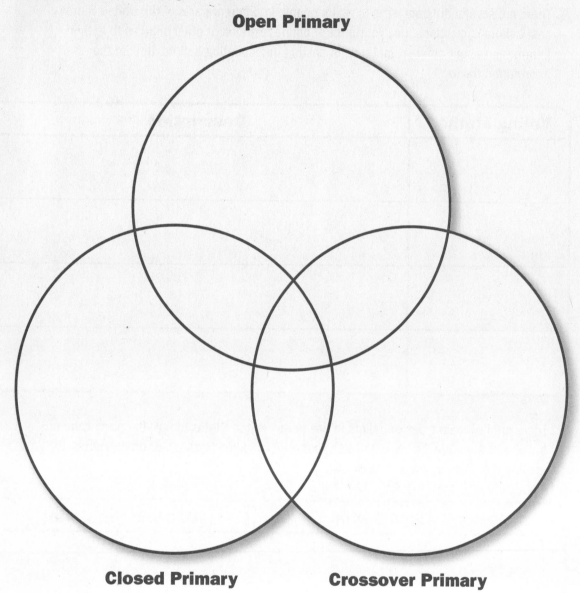

Open Primary

Closed Primary   **Crossover Primary**

👤 What Do You Think?

C. Based on the information above, which method of nominating candidates do you think is the most fair? Which is the most effective? Explain your answers.

_____

_____

_____

_____

CHAPTER 7 How fair and effective is the electoral process?

Name: _____

II. Elections

→ Find Out

A. There are several different ways in which people in different parts of the United States cast ballots in elections. Use your print or online textbook or other sources to gather information about different methods of casting and counting ballots. Record the information below.

Voting Method	Description

B. There are two main types of ballots in use in the United States today—the party column ballot and the office group ballot. Use your print or online textbook or other sources to identify the pros and cons of each type.

Party Column Ballot	Office Group Ballot
•	•
•	•
•	•

👤 What Do You Think?

C. Based on the information you have gathered, which type of voting method and ballot design do you think is likely to produce the most fair and effective elections? Explain.

_____

_____

_____

_____

III. Money and Elections

➔ Find Out

A. Running for office in the United States can be costly. Using your print or online textbook or other sources, read about the sources candidates can draw upon for campaign funding. Record the information you find below.

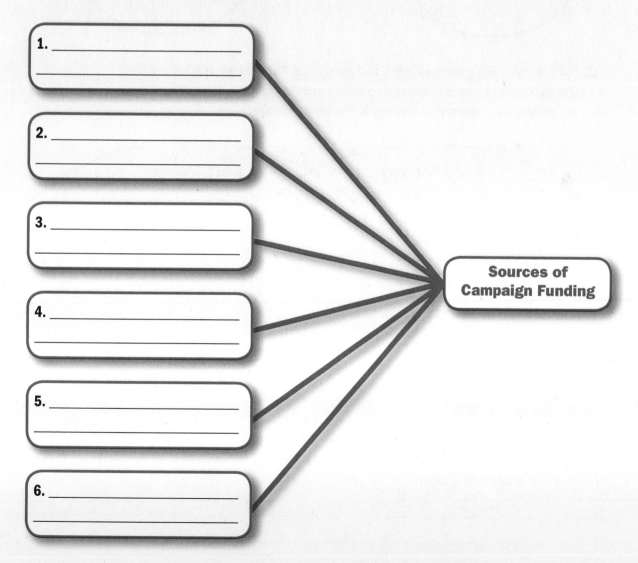

1. _____
   _____

2. _____
   _____

3. _____
   _____

4. _____
   _____

5. _____
   _____

6. _____
   _____

Sources of Campaign Funding

CHAPTER 7 How fair and effective is the electoral process?

Name: _____

B. The Federal Election Commission administers federal election law. Use your print or online textbook or other sources to identify the major functions of this organization, and record the information below.

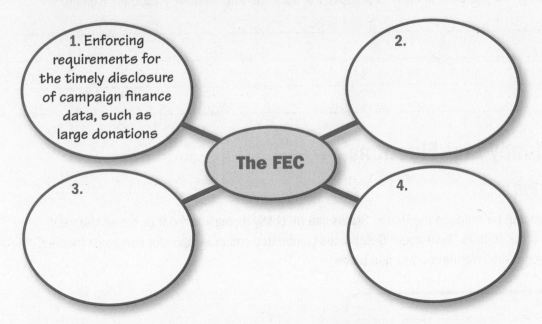

1. Enforcing requirements for the timely disclosure of campaign finance data, such as large donations

2.

The FEC

3.

4.

C. Political fundraising involves two broad categories: hard money and soft money. Use your print or online textbook or other sources to compare and contrast these two categories. Record your findings in the Venn diagram below.

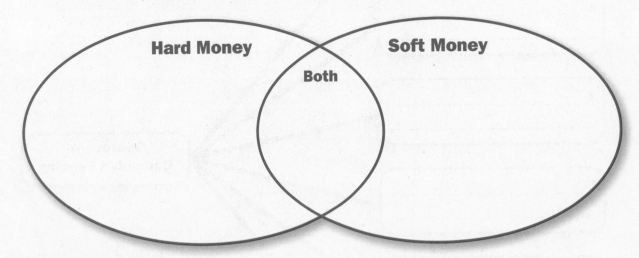

Hard Money

Both

Soft Money

What Do You Think?

D. Based on the information you have gathered, think about the role of money in our electoral process. Explain why money is both essential to fair and effective elections and also a threat to them.

_____

_____

Apply What You've Learned Activity

How does the role of money affect the electoral process and what people think about it? Use this worksheet to answer the Apply What You've Learned activity in your print or online textbook. Use the table below to record your thoughts about the specific questions presented.

What is a compelling argument for and against the following statement: Money is an essential part of the electoral process.	
Describe existing efforts to regulate the role of money in elections.	
Identify the main sources of campaign funding and analyze the impact each source has on elections.	
Analyze the potential effects of removing all money from the process, or of removing all regulation of money.	

A. Do you agree or disagree with the statement that money is an essential part of the electoral process? Explain your answer.

_____

_____

_____

B. Do you think that the fairness of elections and the effectiveness of elections are related? Using your thinking about the role of money in elections, explain how they are similar or different.

_____

_____

_____

_____

Essay

 ## How fair and effective is the electoral process?

Our elections are supposed to express the will of the people. They are supposed to be fair contests that result in effective, responsive government. As you view and read the primary sources below, consider the factors that can impact the fairness and effectiveness of elections.

> Since its inception, the FEC has negotiated the tension between the rights of citizens to enter into political debate and discussion and the need to simultaneously safeguard the integrity of the electoral process.
>
> — *Federal Election Commission*, Thirty-Year Report, *September 2005*

What Do You Think?

What is your opinion? Write a response to the Essential Question, **How fair and effective is the electoral process?** Consider your thoughts on the information above, the Guiding Questions in your textbook, and the activities you have done in your Journal. See page 219 for a rubric on writing an Essential Question essay.

 ## Don't Forget

Your answer to this question will help you think about the Unit 2 Essential Question: **In what ways should people participate in public affairs?**

CHAPTER 8 Mass Media and Public Opinion

Warmup

? **What is the place of the media and public opinion in a democracy?**

A. Think about the ways in which people in our democratic society get information about public issues. Many of these methods are listed below. Which of these do you think has the most significant influence on an individual's opinion? Rank the list below, with 1 being the most influential and 8 being the least influential.

_____ Newspapers

_____ Magazines

_____ Television

_____ The Internet

_____ Radio

_____ Friends

_____ Family

_____ School

B. Which type of media do you think is the most reliable in terms of providing accurate, helpful information on public matters? Explain your answer.

_____

_____

_____

_____

_____

_____

_____

_____

_____

CHAPTER 8 What is the place of the media and public opinion in a democracy?

Name: _____

Exploration

I. The Formation of Public Opinion

→ Find Out

A. Public opinion is influenced by many factors. Using your print or online textbook or other sources, briefly describe how the following factors influence the formation of public opinion.

1. Family _____

_____

2. Education _____

_____

3. Mass Media _____

_____

4. Peer Groups _____

_____

5. Opinion Leaders _____

_____

6. Historical Events _____

_____

● What Do You Think?

B. Think about the factors that influence public opinion listed above. Identify an example of how three of them have influenced your own public opinions or attitudes.

1. _____

_____

_____

2. _____

_____

_____

3. _____

_____

_____

CHAPTER 8 What is the place of the media and public opinion in a democracy?

Name: _____

II. Measuring Public Opinion

→ Find Out

A. Politicians are keenly interested in measuring public opinion. There are a number of ways of doing this, each with its own strengths and limitations. Using your print or online textbook or other sources, record the strengths and limitations of these methods of gauging public opinion.

Methods of Measuring Public Opinion	Strengths	Limitations
Election Results		
Interest Group Activity		
Media Reporting		
Personal Contacts		
Opinion Polls		

B. Opinion polls are the best tool available for testing and measuring public opinion. Yet in order to be effective, a poll must be scientific in its design and execution. Use your print or online textbook or other sources to learn about the steps in creating a scientific public opinion poll. Record your findings in the flowchart below.

1. Define the Universe	2. Construct a Sample	3. Prepare Valid Questions	4. Conduct Interviews	5. Interpret Results
Identify what group's opinion is being measured				

CHAPTER 8 What is the place of the media and public
opinion in a democracy?

Name: _____

What Do You Think?

C. Given the strengths and limitations of different measures of public opinion, how much attention do you think elected officials should pay to "public opinion"? How much attention should they pay, for example, to poll results or letters from constituents?

_____

_____

_____

III. The Mass Media

Find Out

A. Mass media exist in several forms today. Each has its role to play in informing and shaping public opinion. Use your print or online textbook or other sources to provide information about the role of the media as providers of information about public affairs, below.

Type of Mass Media	Key Features
Television	
Newspapers	
Radio	
Magazines	
The Internet	

CHAPTER 8 What is the place of the media and public opinion in a democracy?

Name: _____

B. Use your print or online textbook or other sources to explore the two main ways in which mass media influence our democratic system. Record your findings in the chart below.

Influence of the Media on Politics	
The Public Agenda	**Electoral Politics**

C. Though the mass media are highly influential, a number of factors limit their impact. Use your print or online textbook to explore the reasons why the media's impact is limited. Write your answers in the space below.

Factors that limit the impact of the media on our politics:

1. _____

_____

2. _____

_____

3. _____

_____

4. _____

_____

👤 What Do You Think?

D. What is the role of the mass media in our democracy today?

_____

_____

_____

CHAPTER 8 What is the place of the media and public
opinion in a democracy?

Name: _____

Apply What You've Learned Activity

How influential are the media in your own life? Use this worksheet to record the information
you collect in the Apply What You've Learned questions in your print or online textbook.
Record your use of the media and information about public affairs content of the media
you consume.

Media Used	Public Affairs Content	What You Learned

A. What is your major source of information about public affairs?

_____

B. How often do you seek public affairs information from some form of mass media?

_____

_____

C. Which form of media do you prefer as a source of information (as opposed to
entertainment)? Explain.

_____

_____

_____

CHAPTER 8 What is the place of the media and public opinion in a democracy?

Name: _____

Essay

What is the place of the media and public opinion in a democracy?

In a system of government in which the people rule, public opinion—how it is shaped and influenced—is a matter of great importance. As you read and view the sources below, consider the role of the media and public opinion in our political system.

"That's not my political opinion. That's just stuff I hear on the radio."

> **The force of public opinion cannot be resisted when permitted freely to be expressed. The agitation it produces must be submitted to.**
>
> — *Thomas Jefferson, 1823*

What Do You Think?

What is your opinion? Write a response to the Essential Question, **What is the place of the media and public opinion in a democracy?** Consider your thoughts on the information above, the Guiding Questions in your textbook, and the activities you have done in your Journal. See page 219 for a rubric on writing an Essential Question essay.

Don't Forget

Your answer to this question will help you think about the Unit 2 Essential Question: **In what ways should people participate in public affairs?**

Name: _____

Warmup

 To what extent do interest groups advance or harm democracy?

A. An interest group is defined as any group that seeks to influence public policy. This definition includes a wide range of groups operating at all levels of our political system and society. Identify two examples of interest groups operating in your school and community and what each group hopes to achieve.

- _____
  _____
- _____
  _____

B. Think about what you know about interest groups and their activities. Brainstorm a list of positive and negative terms or ideas that you connect with these groups.

Positive Aspects of Interest Groups

- _____
- _____
- _____

Negative Aspects of Interest Groups

- _____
- _____
- _____

C. The First Amendment to the Constitution guarantees the individual right to "assemble," or to join with others to pursue a common goal. It is this principle that underlies the formation of interest groups in our society. Why do you think that this right was considered so important to the Framers?

_____
_____
_____

CHAPTER 9 To what extent do interest groups advance
or harm democracy?

Name: _____

Exploration

I. The Nature of Interest Groups

Find Out

A. What is an interest group? Use your print or online textbook or other sources to identify
which of the following are interest groups, and which are not.

	Is It an Interest Group?	**Why or Why Not?**
Local police department		
"Neighborhood Watch" Anti-Crime Group		
Local association of business leaders		
Community group for the registration of voters		
Republican Caucus in the legislature		

B. In some respects, interest groups have a very similar role in our political system to
political parties. Yet there are key differences between the two. Use your print or online
textbook or other sources to compare and contrast interest groups and political parties
in our political system.

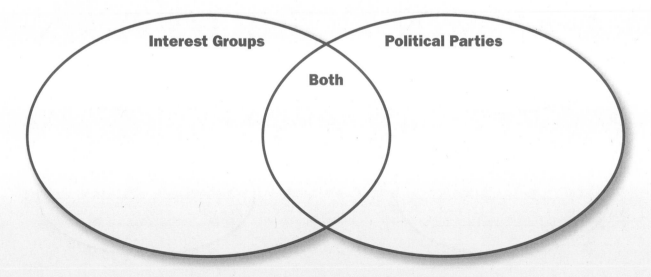

Interest Groups   Both   Political Parties

CHAPTER 9 To what extent do interest groups advance or harm democracy?

Name: _____

C. Interest groups serve valuable functions, yet they are also subject to much criticism. Use your print or online textbook to identify and describe some of the valuable functions and common criticisms of interest groups.

Interest Groups—Good or Bad?	
Valuable Functions	**Common Criticisms**
•	•
•	•
•	•
•	•
•	

👤 What Do You Think?

D. Do the benefits of having interest groups in our system outweigh the drawbacks? Explain.

_____

_____

II. Types of Interest Groups

→ Find Out

A. The most common type of interest group is based on economic interests. Using your print or online textbook or other sources, identify and briefly describe the major categories of these groups in the concept web below.

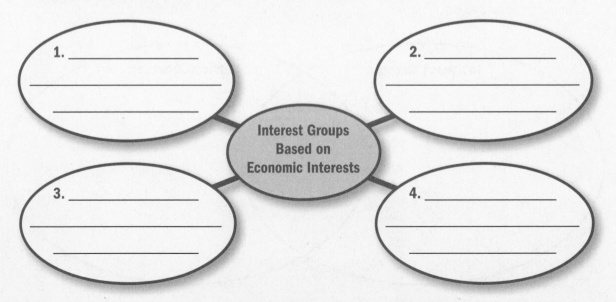

1. _____

_____

_____

2. _____

_____

_____

Interest Groups Based on Economic Interests

3. _____

_____

_____

4. _____

_____

_____

CHAPTER 9 To what extent do interest groups advance or harm democracy?

Name: _____

B. Interest groups can be categorized in several other ways, as well. Use your print or online textbook or other resources to identify and describe some other types of interest groups.

1. _____
_____

2. _____
_____

3. _____
_____

4. _____
_____

👤 What Do You Think?

C. Is there a category of interest group that you think is especially likely to have a positive or negative impact on the political system? Explain your answer.

_____
_____
_____

III. Interest Groups at Work

➔ Find Out

A. Interest groups are defined by their efforts to influence government policy. Use your print or online textbook or other sources to describe how interest groups attempt to influence policy directly in each branch of government.

How Interest Groups Apply Direct Pressure on Government		
Legislative Branch	**Executive Branch**	**Judicial Branch**

CHAPTER 9 To what extent do interest groups advance
or harm democracy?

Name: _____

B. In addition to seeking to influence policy directly, interest groups apply pressure on the policy-making process in indirect ways. Use your print or online textbook or other sources to identify three ways in which interest groups seek to apply indirect pressure.

1. _____

_____

_____

_____

_____

2. _____

_____

_____

_____

_____

3. _____

_____

_____

_____

_____

What Do You Think?

C. In your opinion, does the indirect application of pressure on government by interest groups advance democracy? Explain your answer.

_____

_____

_____

_____

_____

_____

_____

_____

_____

_____

_____

CHAPTER 9 To what extent do interest groups advance or harm democracy?

Name: _____

Apply What You've Learned Activity

Interest groups are at work at all levels of our society—in our communities and in our nation's capital. Use this worksheet to answer the Apply What You've Learned questions in your print or online textbook. Use the table below to record the responses to the following questions:

What are the goals of the interest groups you are studying?	_____ _____ _____
How does each group pursue its goals?	_____ _____ _____
Do you think these groups are effective in their attempts to shape policy?	_____ _____ _____

A. What do you think are the key features in making an interest group effective?

_____

_____

_____

_____

B. Do you think a group can be effective if it does not have the support of the majority of the population? Explain your answer.

_____

_____

_____

_____

_____

CHAPTER 9 To what extent do interest groups advance
or harm democracy?

Name: _____

Essay

 To what extent do interest groups advance or harm democracy?

Since the country was created, observers have worried about the influence of interest groups on the democratic process. As you consider the quotations below, think about the role of interest groups in our society and how they can both promote and interfere with the democratic process.

> By a faction [interest group], I understand a number of citizens, whether amounting to a majority or a minority of the whole, who are united and actuated [made active] by some common impulse of passion, or of interest, adversed to the rights of the other citizens, or to the permanent and aggregate [combined] interests of the community.
>
> — *James Madison,* The Federalist No. 10

> In no country in the world has the principle of association been more successfully used, or more unsparingly applied to a multitude of different objects, than in America.
>
> — *Alexis de Tocqueville,* Democracy in America

What Do You Think?

What is your opinion? Write a response to the Essential Question, **To what extent do interest groups advance or harm democracy?** Consider your thoughts on the quotations above, the Guiding Questions in your textbook, and the activities you have done in your Journal. See page 219 for a rubric on writing an Essential Question essay.

 Don't Forget

Your answer to this question will help you think about the Unit 2 Essential Question: **In what ways should people participate in public affairs?**

Name: _____

UNIT 2 Political Behavior: Government by the People

Essay Warmup

Examine the following perspectives on political participation. The questions that follow each perspective will help you focus your thinking on the Unit 2 Essential Question, **In what ways should people participate in public affairs?**

> Freedom of expression—in particular, freedom of the press—guarantees popular participation in the decisions and actions of government, and popular participation is the essence of . . . democracy.
>
> — *Corazon Aquino, former President of the Philippines*

1. What positive benefit does Aquino believe freedom of expression brings?

_____

_____

2. What does Aquino mean when she says, "popular participation is the essence of . . . democracy"?

_____

_____

> It is not the function of our Government to keep the citizen from falling into error; it is the function of the citizen to keep the Government from falling into error.
>
> — *Justice Robert Houghwout Jackson*, American Communications Association *v.* Douds

3. What does the quote suggest is the function of the citizen in our system?

_____

_____

4. What are some of the ways that citizens can help keep the government from "falling into error"?

_____

_____

_____

Copyright © by Pearson Education, Inc., or its affiliates. All rights reserved.

73

"I'm undecided, but that doesn't mean I'm apathetic or uninformed."

5. Who do you think has called the man in the cartoon?

_____

_____

6. What does the man mean by what he is saying to the caller?

_____

_____

7. What is the main idea of this cartoon? Do you agree or disagree?

_____

_____

What Do You Think?

8. Choose one of the documents above and explain how it helps you answer the Unit 2 Essential Question, **In what ways should people participate in public affairs?**

_____

_____

_____

_____

UNIT 2 Political Behavior: Government by the People

Essay

 In what ways should people participate in public affairs?

Write an essay that answers the Essential Question, **In what ways should people participate in public affairs?** Use your answers to the Essential Question warmup questions on the previous pages, your answers to the chapter Essential Questions, and what you have learned in this unit. Keep in mind that your essay should reflect your thoughtful and well-supported personal point of view. Answering the prompts below will help you structure your essay. Go to page 219 for a rubric for writing an Essential Question essay.

Thesis Statement: _____

_____

Body Paragraph 1	Body Paragraph 2	Body Paragraph 3
Main Idea	**Main Idea**	**Main Idea**
_____	_____	_____
_____	_____	_____
_____	_____	_____
_____	_____	_____
Supporting Details	**Supporting Details**	**Supporting Details**
1. _____	1. _____	1. _____
_____	_____	_____
_____	_____	_____
2. _____	2. _____	2. _____
_____	_____	_____
_____	_____	_____
3. _____	3. _____	3. _____
_____	_____	_____

Conclusion: _____

_____

Unit 3

The Legislative Branch

 Essential Question

What makes a successful Congress?

Chapter 10
Essential Question

Whose views should members of Congress represent when voting?

Chapter 11
Essential Question

What should be the limits on the powers of Congress?

Chapter 12
Essential Question

Can and should the lawmaking process be improved?

UNIT 3 The Legislative Branch

Warmup

The United States House of Representatives

What makes a successful Congress?

Congress passes laws that directly influence the daily lives of the more than 300 million people in the United States and, often, affect the entire world. It has enormous power. How should that power be used? In Unit 3, you will study Congress and explore possible answers to the Essential Question above.

A. Below is a list of standards for judging a successful Congress. Check the three that are most important to you. Mark an X in the box of three that are least important to you.

☐ Balances the budget

☐ Is careful not to overstep its constitutional powers

☐ Works well with the President

☐ Passes a lot of laws intended to solve national problems

☐ Emphasizes the importance of representing individual districts and States

☐ Works together despite party differences

☐ Focuses on global issues as well as issues that only affect the United States

☐ Is controlled by one party in the House and the other in the Senate

☐ Is controlled by one party in both the House and the Senate

☐ Represents a wide variety of opinions

☐ Has a lot of experienced members

☐ Gets a high percentage of its members reelected

☐ Helps people who have problems with government agencies

☐ Creates a lot of new jobs

☐ Lowers the national debt

☐ Closely reflects popular opinion

☐ Compromises to get things done

B. Explain why you chose your top three standards for judging Congress.

_____

_____

Warmup

 ## Whose views should members of Congress represent when voting?

How should members of Congress balance the needs and wishes of both the people they represent and other people in government? Rank the following interests on the scales from not important to very important.

A. Voters in his or her district (for House members)

Not Important ▸ ☐☐☐☐☐☐☐☐☐ Very Important ▸

Explain your ranking.

_____

_____

B. All residents of the State from which he or she was elected (Senate members)

Not Important ▸ ☐☐☐☐☐☐☐☐☐ Very Important ▸

Explain your ranking. _____

_____

C. The nation as a whole

Not Important ▸ ☐☐☐☐☐☐☐☐☐ Very Important ▸

Explain your ranking. _____

_____

D. His or her political party

Not Important ▸ ☐☐☐☐☐☐☐☐☐ Very Important ▸

Explain your ranking. _____

_____

CHAPTER 10 Whose views should members of Congress represent when voting?

Name: _____

Exploration

I. Representation and Bicameralism

→ Find Out

A. Use your print or online textbook to find the reasons why the Framers of the U.S. Constitution specified a bicameral legislature. Use that information to complete the statements below.

■ The House has 435 members; the Senate has _____ members. Why is there a difference in the number of members in each house?

_____

_____

■ Senators have six-year terms. Representatives have _____-year terms. What effect do you think the difference in the length of terms has on the way senators and representatives vote?

_____

_____

■ Representatives represent a district within a State. Senators represent _____. What influence do you think this difference has on the interests of senators and representatives?

_____

_____

● What Do You Think?

B. Representatives have always been chosen by the people, but until 1913, senators were chosen by State legislatures. In 1913, the 17th Amendment changed the method by which senators were elected to election by the people. Do you think the Framers would have approved of this change? Do you think senators vote differently than they did due to this change? Explain.

_____

_____

_____

_____

CHAPTER 10 Whose views should members of Congress represent when voting?

Name: _____

II. Approaches to Representation

→ Find Out

A. Use your print or online textbook to review different approaches that congressional representatives can take in making decisions. Then complete the following activities. Draw a line from each term on the left to its correct description on the right.

delegate   votes according to the wishes of his or her party's leaders

partisan   juggles the concerns of constituents, the wishes of the party leadership, his or her own views, and the political pressures of the moment

politico   decides how to vote based on his or her own judgment on the issue

trustee   casts each vote to represent the views of constituents

⊙ What Do You Think?

B. Rank the four basic approaches to representation from the one you would most like your own representatives in Congress to use to the one you would least like them to use.

1 _____

2 _____

3 _____

4 _____

C. Explain the reasons for your ranking, including how you would like your own representative to vote.

_____

_____

_____

_____

_____

_____

_____

Name: _____

III. Reapportionment

→ Find out

A. What does *reapportionment* mean? When and why does it occur?

_____

_____

_____

B. Use your print or online textbook to complete a time line of major changes in the House of Representatives due to reapportionment.

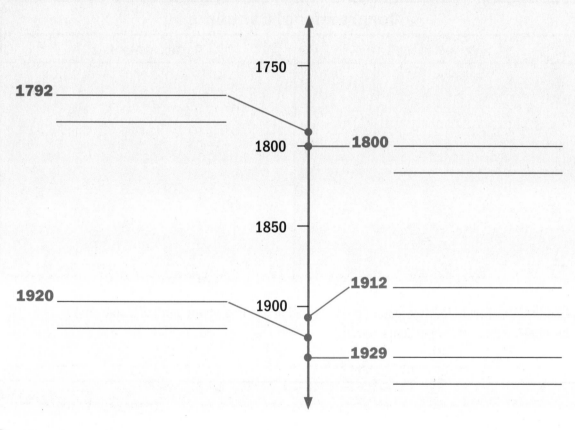

👤 What Do You Think?

C. What was the reasoning behind passage of the Reapportionment Act of 1929? Do you think that this law makes the representation in the House more or less fair than it had been previously? Explain.

_____

_____

_____

_____

CHAPTER 10 Whose views should members of Congress represent when voting?

Name: _____

Apply What You've Learned Activity

What impact do earmarks have on the relationship between members of Congress and their constituents? What impact do they have on the nation as a whole? Use this worksheet to organize answers to the Apply What You've Learned questions in your print or online textbook.

A. Complete the table below with arguments for and against earmarks. Draw a circle around the arguments in the table that you find most persuasive. (*Note:* You may find that you agree with some points made by each side.)

Congressional Earmarks	
Arguments For	**Arguments Against**

B. Use the flowchart below to organize the information you find about earmarks sponsored by your congressional representatives.

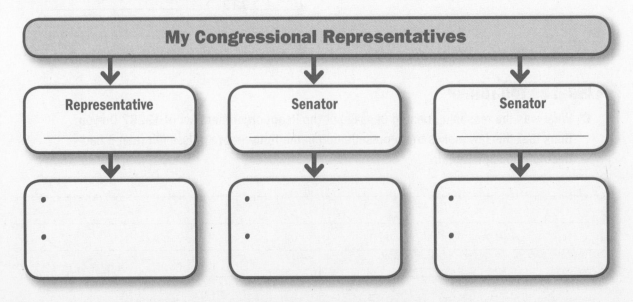

CHAPTER 10 Whose views should members of Congress represent when voting?

Name: _____

Essay

Whose views should members of Congress represent when voting?

The Framers designed a representative democracy when they wrote the Constitution, but the question of how Americans can best be represented has been debated ever since. Keeping in mind the different views of representation you have studied in this chapter, analyze the poll data presented below.

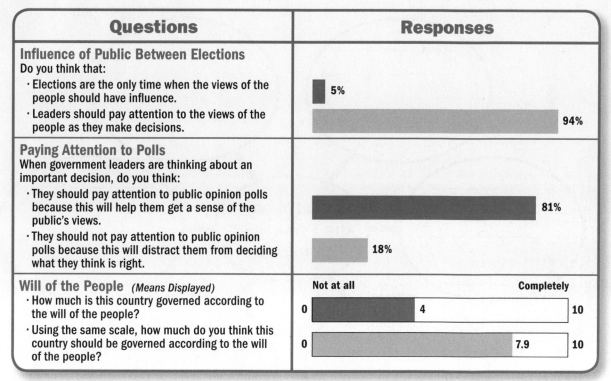

Questions	Responses
Influence of Public Between Elections Do you think that: · Elections are the only time when the views of the people should have influence. · Leaders should pay attention to the views of the people as they make decisions.	5% 94%
Paying Attention to Polls When government leaders are thinking about an important decision, do you think: · They should pay attention to public opinion polls because this will help them get a sense of the public's views. · They should not pay attention to public opinion polls because this will distract them from deciding what they think is right.	81% 18%
Will of the People *(Means Displayed)* · How much is this country governed according to the will of the people? · Using the same scale, how much do you think this country should be governed according to the will of the people?	Not at all — Completely 0 ... 4 ... 10 0 ... 7.9 ... 10

Source: WorldPublicOpinion.org

What Do You Think?

What is your own opinion? Write a response to the Essential Question, **Whose views should members of Congress represent when voting?** Consider your thoughts on the poll data presented above, the Guiding Questions in your textbook, and the activities you have completed in your Journal. See page 219 for a rubric on writing an Essential Question essay.

Don't Forget

Your answer to this question will help you think about the Unit 3 Essential Question: **What makes a successful Congress?**

Warmup

 What should be the limits on the powers of Congress?

A. Why might people want to place limits on the powers of Congress? Are there disadvantages to such limits? Complete the concept web below with your ideas.

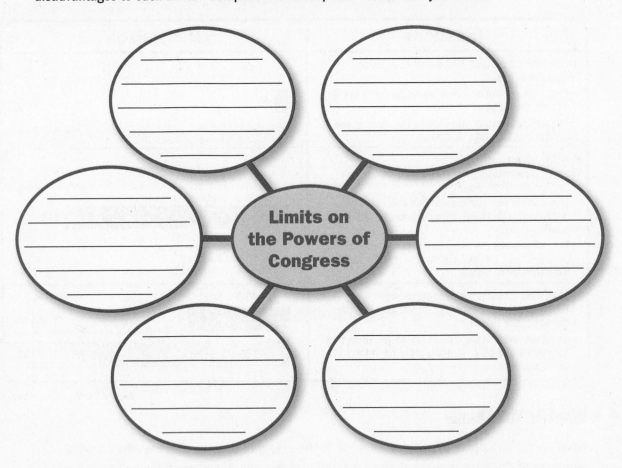

Limits on
the Powers of
Congress

B. Are limits on the powers of Congress less important or more important today than they were in 1787? Explain your answer.

_____

_____

_____

_____

_____

Exploration

I. The Six Basic Principles

➡ Find Out

A. Use your print or online textbook to find information about the six principles on which the U.S. Constitution is based. Then complete the table, below.

Six Basic Principles	
Principle	**Description**
Federalism	Power is divided between the Federal Government and the States.

👤 What Do You Think?

B. Use your prior knowledge and what you have learned about government to give a present-day example of each of the six principles at work.

limited government

Six Basic Principles

U.S. Supreme Court rules D.C. handgun ban unconstitutional.

II. Powers of Congress

→ Find Out

A. Review Article I, sections 8 and 9 of the U.S. Constitution, your print or online textbook, or other sources on the powers of Congress. Circle the three powers in the list below that you think are the most important. Then describe the limits, if any, that are placed by Article I on each power listed.

Limits on the Powers of Congress	
Commerce	
Taxation	
Bankruptcy	
Borrowing	
Currency	
Foreign Policy	
War	
Postal	
Copyrights and Patents	
Weights and Measures	
Territories and Lands	
Eminent Domain	can take private property only for public use
Naturalization	
Judicial	

👤 What Do You Think?

B. Are the limits that the Constitution places on the powers of Congress too narrow, too broad, or about right in today's world? Explain your answer on another sheet of paper.

III. Constitutional Interpretation

➔ Find Out

A. Review the constitutional debate over strict and liberal construction in your print or online textbook or other sources. Use the table below to organize information about strict and liberal constructionists.

Features	Strict Constructionists	Liberal Constructionists
Leader		
Goals		
View of National Government		broad view of the National Government's powers
View of Implied Powers	Implied powers are only those absolutely necessary to carrying out the expressed powers.	

B. Review the implied powers of Congress. Then read each of the following statements about the case of *McCulloch* v. *Maryland*. If it is true, write T in the blank; if it is false, write F.

____ 1. This case involved the power of a State government to tax the Federal Government.

____ 2. The Supreme Court ruled in favor of McCulloch.

____ 3. Strict constructionists favored the National Bank.

____ 4. This case was a victory for liberal constructionists.

____ 5. The Court based its decision largely on the Necessary and Proper Clause.

____ 6. The phrase "the power to tax involves the power to destroy" in the Court's decision was a reference to the constitutional limits on the powers of Congress.

👤 What Do You Think?

C. Why was *McCulloch* v. *Maryland* a landmark case in constitutional law?

_____

_____

_____

Apply What You've Learned Activity

What impact has liberal construction of the U.S. Constitution had on the powers of Congress? Use this worksheet to organize answers to the Apply What You've Learned questions in your print or online textbook.

A. Use the table below to organize your answers to the Apply What You've Learned Questions in your print or online textbook.

Constitutional Limits	Under Strict Construction
Limit 1	
Limit 2	
Limit 3	

B. Write your answer to question 13 in your print or online textbook, below.

_____

_____

_____

_____

_____

C. As you consider how to answer question 13 from your print or online textbook, compare the arguments that could be made by those who say Yes or No. Use the table below to organize a list of arguments each side might make.

Has the Elastic Clause been stretched too far?	
Yes, it has	No, it hasn't
The balance between Federal and State powers has been upset.	The country faces many challenges today that the Framers could not foresee.

Essay

What should be the limits on the powers of Congress?

When the strict constructionists and liberal constructionists debated the powers of Congress and what limits should be placed on it, they wanted a government powerful enough to hold the nation together, yet not powerful enough to take away the freedom and rights of the States or of the people.

> I consider the foundation of the Constitution as laid on this ground: That 'all powers not delegated to the United States, by the Constitution, nor prohibited by it to the States, are reserved to the States or to the people.' To take a single step beyond the boundaries thus specifically drawn around the powers of Congress, is to take possession of a boundless field of power, no longer susceptible to any definition.
>
> — *Thomas Jefferson, 1791*

> Constitutions should consist only of general provisions; the reason is that they must necessarily be permanent, and that they cannot calculate for the possible change of things.
>
> — *Alexander Hamilton, Speech to the New York Constitutional Convention, 1788*

🧑 What Do You Think?

What is your opinion? Write a response to the Essential Question, **What should be the limits on the powers of Congress?** Consider your thoughts on the quotations above, the Guiding Questions in your textbook, and the activities you have done in your Journal. See page 219 for a rubric on writing an Essential Question essay.

Don't Forget

Your answer to this question will help you think about the Unit 3 Essential Question: **What makes a successful Congress?**

Warmup

 ## Can and should the lawmaking process be improved?

A. What are Congress' most important duties and responsibilities? Consider the list below. Add any job you think should be included. Then circle the three jobs you think are the most important.

■ Overseeing executive branch

■ Investigating wrongdoing

■ Evaluating proposals for and passing laws

■ Approving treaties with foreign nations

■ Amending the Constitution

■ Appropriating federal funds

■ Helping constituents deal with the federal bureaucracy

■ Bringing federal projects and money to members' States or districts

■ Impeachment and trial of federal officials

■ Representing the people of members' States or districts

■ Electing President or Vice President under unusual circumstances

■ Approving presidential appointments

■ Other: _____

■ Other: _____

■ Other: _____

B. Explain why you chose the three jobs circled above.

_____

_____

_____

_____

_____

Exploration

I. Organization of Congress

➔ Find Out

A. Read about congressional organization in your print or online textbook or other sources. Then complete this chart by listing the officers in each house and a brief description of the duties of each.

SENATE
Presiding Officers
Vice President
_____
Party Officers
Majority Leader   Minority Leader
Majority Whip   Minority Whip

HOUSE
Presiding Officer
_____
Party Officers
Majority Leader   Minority Leader
Majority Whip   Minority Whip

B. What is the seniority rule? What are some pros and cons of this system?

_____
_____
_____

C. What changes have been made to the seniority rule in recent years?

_____
_____

👤 What Do You Think?

D. Do you think the reliance on seniority is good or bad for Congress and for the country? Explain.

_____
_____

II. The Work of Committees

→ Find Out

A. Read in your print or online textbook about how bills are assigned to committee. How can the authors of a bill try to influence its assignment? Who makes the assignment? What options does the assigner have?

_____

_____

_____

_____

_____

B. Standing committees have great power to control what bills become laws under their jurisdictions. Read about committees in Congress in your print or online textbook or other sources. Then use the organizer below to list the options a committee has when it votes on the status of a bill, and describe circumstances under which each option might be used.

Option	Description	Circumstances
1.		
2.	refuse to report bill	
3.		
4.		
5.		None of the proposed bills was adequate.

C. Congress has developed several types of committees to serve different purposes. Use the table below to organize information about the four types of committees.

	Standing	Joint	Conference	Select
Members From		both houses of Congress		
Operating Time Frame				usually temporary
Purpose				

👤 What Do You Think?

D. What problem(s) was the committee system designed to solve? Are there drawbacks to the committee system as it now exists? Are there changes that could be made that would improve the system? Explain your answers.

_____

_____

_____

_____

_____

III. Making Laws

⮞ Find Out

A. Review the lawmaking process in your print or online textbook or other sources. Then use the flowchart below to map the progress of a bill through the House. At each point, use the margin to jot down your questions and thoughts about the process.

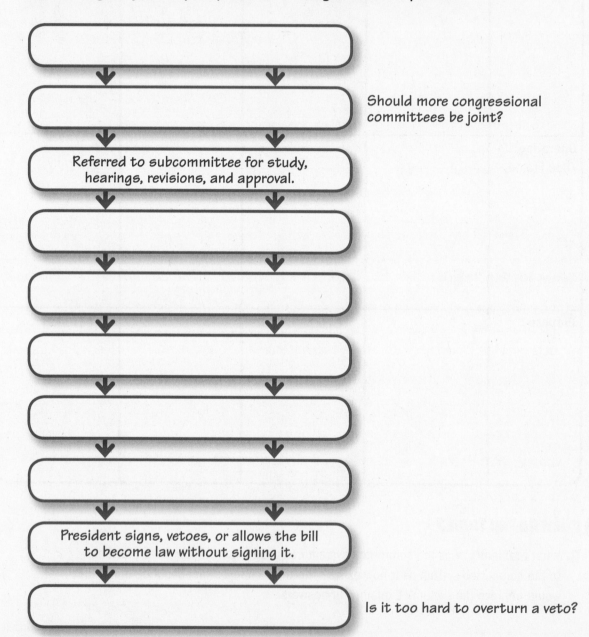

Should more congressional committees be joint?

Referred to subcommittee for study, hearings, revisions, and approval.

President signs, vetoes, or allows the bill to become law without signing it.

Is it too hard to overturn a veto?

⬤ What Do You Think?

B. As you have learned, very few bills become law. Do you think it might be worthwhile to reduce the time Congress spends drafting, defending, and reviewing so many doomed bills? If so, how? If not, why not? Answer on a separate sheet of paper.

IV. Debate in the Senate

➔ Find Out

A. The Senate has a longstanding tradition of unlimited debate, which was intended to foster careful consideration of every issue. Review your print or online textbook and other sources to learn about debate in the Senate. Then mark each statement below with a T or an F to show if you think it is true or false.

____ 1. The Constitution guarantees unlimited debate in the Senate.

____ 2. The purpose of a filibuster is to delay or defeat a measure that would pass if put to a vote.

____ 3. The "two-speech rule" is a mechanism to make filibustering easier.

____ 4. The cloture rule was passed after a World-War-I-era filibuster that outraged the public and the President.

____ 5. Cloture requires a two-thirds vote of the Senate.

____ 6. Filibusters have become common in recent years.

👤 What Do You Think?

B. There are both advantages and disadvantages to the filibuster. Use the table to list its pros and cons. Then write a statement explaining your view on this question: Is the filibuster an outmoded institution or an important tradition that should be preserved?

The Filibuster	
Pros	**Cons**
can prevent hasty decision-making	

_____

_____

_____

_____

_____

_____

V. Compare and Contrast the House and Senate

→ Find Out

A. Review your print or online textbook or other sources on differences between the House and the Senate. Then put an S before the statement below if it applies mainly to the Senate and an H before it if it applies mainly to the House.

____ Great power for committee chairs	____ Less power for committee chairs
____ Shorter terms of office	____ Longer terms of office
____ Complex rules	____ Informal rules
____ Almost unlimited debate	____ Limited debate
____ Great power for presiding officer	____ Less power for presiding officer
____ Always introduces tax bills	____ Never introduces tax bills
____ Continuous body	____ Reconstitutes itself each term

Write a short summary of the differences between the House and Senate.

_____

_____

_____

_____

_____

_____

_____

_____

_____

👤 What Do You Think?

B. Write three reasons why Congress does not always work with the greatest speed and efficiency. Then answer the following question: Should Congress work with greater speed and efficiency? Explain your answer.

_____

_____

_____

_____

_____

Apply What You've Learned Activity

As you have learned, real lawmaking does not always follow the neat steps depicted in textbook charts of the process. Use the graphic organizers and questions below to help you record your research and complete the Apply What You've Learned Activity in your print or online textbook.

A. Summarize information about the two recent bills you chose for your activity. You may consider looking for bills on the legislative information Web site from the Library of Congress, known as "Thomas."

	Bill 1	Bill 2
Official Number		
Short Title		
Sponsor		
Purpose		
Final Status		

B. On a separate sheet of paper, draw simple flowcharts to illustrate the progress of your two bills. Add as many steps as you need to for each bill.

C. Which stages progressed well for each bill? At which stages, if any, did each bill do poorly?

_____

_____

_____

_____

_____

D. Write your answer to question 12 from your print or online textbook, below. Use additional sheets of paper as necessary.

_____

_____

_____

_____

Essay

 ## Can and should the lawmaking process be improved?

Each house of Congress makes its own process rules and is free to change them *"within the limits of the Constitution."* In addition, the Framers provided ways to amend the U.S. Constitution, if necessary. As you think about your answer to the Chapter Essential Question, consider the observations of two congressional scholars describing what Congress should do.

> If I could do one thing procedurally to heal the House and Senate and begin to restore some semblance of its deliberative role, I would . . . force it into a two weeks on/two weeks off schedule. . . . They would spend more time around their colleagues, seeing them as human beings and not as the enemy.
>
> — *Norman Ornstein,* Want to Fix Congress?

> Extensive debate is written into the very structure of our congressional system. At every level [in Congress], . . . there is the presumption of discussion, debate, disagreement and even argument. Our Founders understood the importance of conflict in the system, both as a way for all views to be represented, and as a process for building common ground among them.
>
> — *Lee Hamilton,* Debate Is Good For Our System

What Do You Think?

What is your opinion? Write a response to the Essential Question, **Can and should the lawmaking process be improved?** Consider your thoughts on the quotations above, the Guiding Questions in your textbook, and the activities you have done in your Journal. See page 219 for a rubric on writing an Essential Question essay.

 ### Don't Forget

Your answer to this question will help you think about the Unit 3 Essential Question: **What makes a successful Congress?**

UNIT 3 The Legislative Branch

Essay Warmup

Examine the following perspectives on the work of Congress. The questions that follow each perspective will help you focus your thinking on the Unit 3 Essential Question, **What makes a successful Congress?**

> Congress should pass laws that reflect the will of the people; that is, Congress should be responsive to popular majorities. Congress should pass laws that deal promptly and effectively with pressing national problems. These two criteria, which can be labeled responsiveness and responsibility, are distinct. Only in a perfect world would what the majority wants always accord with what policy experts deem most likely to be effective. When a conflict exists, which should take priority?
>
> — *Barbara Sinclair, UCLA*

1. How would *you* answer the question of which should take priority—responsiveness or responsibility? Explain.

_____

_____

> . . . Congress simply isn't set up to be efficient. It moves by inches for a very good reason—it was designed for deliberation, not speed. . . . The truth is, Congress deals with the toughest issues in the country. Its job is to understand them thoroughly, weigh the beliefs and interests of an astounding variety of Americans, and consider carefully how to move forward. Passion and speed are not conducive to good legislation; on the whole, we want to use the brakes on the process provided by the Constitution and by congressional structure.
>
> — *Lee Hamilton, Indiana University and 34-year veteran of the House*

2. Do you think Hamilton would agree with Professor Sinclair that Americans want a Congress that will "deal promptly and effectively with pressing national problems"? Explain.

_____

_____

3. Study the cartoon and answer the following questions:

   a. What do the donkey and the elephant in this picture represent?

_____

_____

   b. What do the paint fight and the word balloons coming out of the animals' mouths suggest?

_____

_____

4. What point is the cartoonist making?

_____

_____

👤 What Do You Think?

5. Choose one of the documents above and explain how it helps you answer the Unit 3 Essential Question, **What makes a successful Congress?**

_____

_____

_____

_____

_____

UNIT 3 The Legislative Branch

Essay

 What makes a successful Congress?

Write an essay that answers the Essential Question, **What makes a successful Congress?**
Use your answers to the Essential Question warmup questions on the previous pages, your
answers to the chapter Essential Questions, and what you have learned in this unit. Keep in
mind that your essay should reflect your thoughtful and well-supported point of view. Filling
in the chart below will help you structure your essay. Go to page 219 for a rubric on writing
an Essential Question essay.

Thesis Statement: _____

_____

Body Paragraph 1	Body Paragraph 2	Body Paragraph 3
Main Idea	**Main Idea**	**Main Idea**
_____	_____	_____
_____	_____	_____
_____	_____	_____
_____	_____	_____
Supporting Details	**Supporting Details**	**Supporting Details**
1. _____	1. _____	1. _____
_____	_____	_____
_____	_____	_____
2. _____	2. _____	2. _____
_____	_____	_____
_____	_____	_____
3. _____	3. _____	3. _____

Conclusion: _____

_____

Unit 4

The Executive Branch

Essential Question

What makes a good President?

Chapter 13
Essential Question

Does the current electoral process result in the best candidates for President?

Chapter 14
Essential Question

How much power should the President have?

Chapter 15
Essential Question

Is the bureaucracy essential to good government?

Chapter 16
Essential Question

How should the federal budget reflect Americans' priorities?

Chapter 17
Essential Question

How should the United States interact with other countries?

UNIT 4 The Executive Branch

Warmup

President Lyndon Johnson (1963–1969)

What makes a good President?

The President of the United States leads the world's richest, mightiest country. For that reason, the person who holds the presidency must be able to handle both vast power and massive pressure. In Unit 4, you will explore the scope of this remarkable job and consider the possible answers to the Essential Question above.

A. What qualities must a President have? Review the list of leadership qualities. Then check the top five most important.

☐ thoughtful   ☐ cooperative   ☐ brave

☐ outgoing   ☐ modest   ☐ decent

☐ charming   ☐ kind   ☐ well-informed

☐ trustworthy   ☐ consistent   ☐ independent

☐ decisive   ☐ inspiring   ☐ diplomatic

☐ intelligent   ☐ experienced   ☐ farsighted

☐ tough   ☐ honest   ☐ other _____

☐ open minded   ☐ politically astute

B. Choose a past or current President. What five categories from the list above best describe this President? Explain your choice.

_____

_____

_____

_____

_____

Name: _____

Warmup

 Does the current electoral process result in the best candidates for President?

A. What factors make the best candidate for President? Review the qualifications of four fictional candidates for the presidency below. Circle the four you think are most important.

Candidate A
• attended a top-name college • worked as a lawyer for 15 years • cancer survivor

Candidate C
• was a professor of political science at a top-name university • was most recently governor of a large East Coast State • father of four children

Candidate B
• served three terms in the U.S. Senate • has a business degree and was the founder of a major international company • previously an actor

Candidate D
• served in the Persian Gulf War • was most recently commander of American troops in Afghanistan • lives in Montana

B. Based on the qualifications you chose, place an X beside the category below that you find to be the most important for a presidential candidate. Then explain your answer.

____ Education ____ Political experience

____ Career choice ____ Other _____

____ Military experience

What is your reasoning for selecting that category?

_____

_____

_____

CHAPTER 13 Does the current electoral process result in the best candidates for President?

Name: _____

Exploration

I. The President's Job Description

➔ Find Out

A. Read Article II, Section 1, Clause 5 of the Constitution. Then list the three qualifications an individual must meet to be President of the United States.

1. _____

2. _____

3. _____

Why do you think there are so few formal qualifications?

_____

_____

_____

_____

B. The candidate who wins the presidency must fulfill eight basic roles. Review the presidential roles in your print or online textbook and list them with a brief description of each in the table below. Then read all of Article II of the Constitution and cite the location where each role is mentioned. Circle the two roles you think are the most important.

Presidential Role	Description	Constitution
chief of state	ceremonial head of the U.S. government	Article II, Section 1, Clause 1

CHAPTER 13   Does the current electoral process result
in the best candidates for President?

Name: _____

Why do you think those two roles are the most important?

_____

_____

👤 What Do You Think?

C. The job of President is very complex and demanding. Keeping in mind the roles that the President must fulfill, what do you think are the three most important qualifications or characteristics a candidate must have to be a good President? Explain your reasoning.

_____

_____

_____

_____

_____

_____

II. The Vice Presidency

➡ Find Out

A. Review the role of the Vice President and the manner in which he or she is selected in your print or online textbook or other sources. Then summarize your findings below.

_____

_____

_____

👤 What Do You Think?

B. The Vice President is first in line to succeed the President and therefore "only a heartbeat away from the presidency." However, the individual selected for the vice presidency is often chosen largely to help the presidential candidate win the office. Do you think the manner in which the Vice President is selected results in the best candidates for the office? Why or why not?

_____

_____

_____

_____

_____

Name: _____

III. Presidential Selection and Nomination

➔ Find Out

A. To understand the American electoral system, one needs to understand the history behind its creation. Using your print or online textbook or other sources, review the original provisions the Framers made for selecting presidential electors. Then, in the space below, summarize the method as originally created by the Framers.

_____

_____

_____

_____

B. The rise of political parties and the election of 1800 led to the 12th Amendment. What one significant change did this amendment make to the electoral college system?

_____

_____

➔ What Do You Think?

C. The Framers believed that the presidential electors would act as "free agents" in the election process. The election of 1800 proved that political parties greatly affected this belief. Should presidential electors cast their votes in line with a political party? Why or why not?

_____

_____

_____

_____

➔ Find Out

D. What two methods do States use to select delegates to the national conventions? Circle the one that is used most commonly among the States. Indicate next to each method the State that is scheduled first in that method.

_____ **1.** _____

_____ **2.** _____

E. In the two methods you listed above, for whom do the voters in a presidential election actually vote?

_____

CHAPTER 13 Does the current electoral process result
in the best candidates for President?

Name: _____

What Do You Think?

F. Many States today are trying to get their primaries or caucuses scheduled as early as possible. Reflect on the campaigning process at this stage of the presidential race. Do you think that the presidential election system would be improved if all the States voted on the same day or within a relatively short timeframe? Explain your reasoning.

_____

_____

→ Find Out

G. Both the Republican and Democratic national conventions follow the same basic schedule. Complete the concept web below with the key events that occur during these conventions.

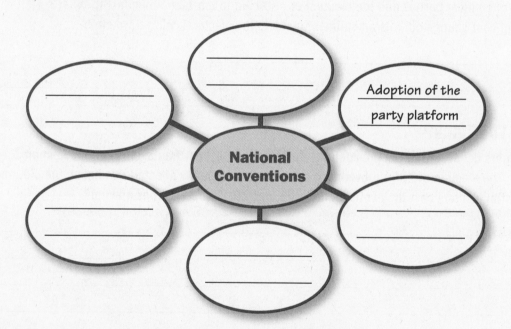

National Conventions

Adoption of the party platform

IV. Presidential Campaign and Election

What Do You Think?

A. The media has, at times, been criticized for obvious favoritism for one candidate over another. In fact, some newspapers publicize who they are backing in the race. Do you think the public backing of the media and other influential sources has an effect on the voting public? Why or why not?

_____

_____

_____

_____

CHAPTER 13 Does the current electoral process result
in the best candidates for President?

Name: _____

➡ Find Out

B. Although most Americans think the presidential election is one event, there are actually
several steps involved. Use the graphic organizer below to track the events that must
occur before the President and Vice President are officially elected.

> On the Tuesday after the first Monday in November, electors
> are chosen by popular election in every State.

⬇

⬇

⬇

⬇

C. The electoral college system has been criticized over the years, and several reforms to
the system have been proposed. Using your print or online textbook, list the three major
flaws of the electoral college system, below, and then indicate the system you think
would be the best method for electing the President. Explain your reasoning.

Flaw 1 _____

Flaw 2 _____

Flaw 3 _____

Best Method:

_____

_____

👤 What Do You Think?

D. Of all the methods available to elect a President, including the electoral college system,
which one do you think is the most fair and democratic? Explain your reasoning.

_____

_____

_____

CHAPTER 13 Does the current electoral process result in the best candidates for President?

Name: _____

Apply What You've Learned Activity

How well did the presidential election system work for your State in the last election? Use this worksheet to answer the Apply What You've Learned questions in your print or online textbook. Conduct research on the primary/caucus results in your State for the most recent presidential election. Use the space below to record your findings.

1. Which method of delegate selection was used? _____

2. Where in the election schedule did your State's primary/caucus fall?

    early   middle   late   Date: _____

3. How many candidates were in the running at the time? _____

    Names: _____

_____

4. What percentage of your State's population voted in the primary/caucus?

    Total number of primary/caucus voters: _____

    Total State population: _____

    Percentage of State population that voted: _____

5. What percentage of your State's population voted in the presidential election?

    Total number of presidential election voters: _____

    Total State population: _____

    Percentage of State population that voted: _____

6. Did your State's electoral college vote reflect the results of its popular election? _____

    A. Do you think the placement on the election schedule affected the turnout for your State's primary/caucus? Explain.

    _____

    _____

    _____

    B. Look back at the flaws of the electoral college that you listed in Part IV.C. Do the results of your research reflect any of the issues that are considered flaws in the system? If so, list the issue and relative flaw below.

    Election result issue _____

    Election system flaw _____

CHAPTER 13 Does the current electoral process result in the best candidates for President?

Name: _____

Essay

Does the current electoral process result in the best candidates for President?

The Constitution places few limits on the qualifications necessary to run for President. Considering the expensive and grueling process of the campaign system, is it possible that the best candidates may not actually make it through to the presidential election? As you review the perspectives below, consider to what extent the election process results in the best candidates for President.

> A President needs political understanding to *run* the government, but he may be *elected* without it.
>
> — *Harry S Truman*

> In every election in American history both parties have their clichés. The party that has the clichés that ring true wins.
>
> — *Newt Gingrich, 1988*

 ## What Do You Think?

What is your opinion? Write a response to the Essential Question, **Does the current electoral process result in the best candidates for President?** Consider your thoughts on the quotations above, the Guiding Questions in your textbook, and the activities you have done in your Journal. See page 219 for a rubric on writing an Essential Question essay.

 ## Don't Forget

Your answer to this question will help you think about the Unit 4 Essential Question: **What makes a good President?**

CHAPTER **14** The Presidency in Action

Warmup

How much power should the President have?

A. What does the word *power* mean to you? Fill in the concept web below to clarify your thinking. Then circle any of the powers you listed that you think a U.S. President should have.

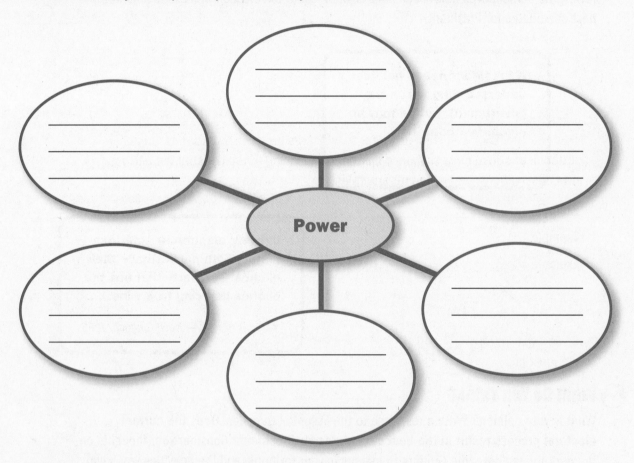

Power

B. Where would you place an ideal U.S. President on a scale of power? Explain your answer.

_____

_____

| No Real Power | | | | | | | | | | | Absolute Power |

Exploration

I. Article II, Growth of Presidential Power

→ Find Out

A. Read Article II of the Constitution. Then make a list of the most important powers that the Constitution gives to the President.

1. _____

2. _____

3. _____

4. _____

5. _____

B. The power of the President has greatly increased since the Constitution was written. Find two examples of increases in the power of the President in your print or online textbook or other sources. Then, based on your reading of the Constitution and your own observations, add two more examples.

Example _____

Example _____

Example _____

Example _____

C. Review the reasons for the growth of presidential power and list them below. Then circle the most important reason and explain your choice.

_____

_____

_____

_____

_____

_____

_____

_____

_____

What Do You Think?

D. Has the power of the President grown too much? Choose an example from the news or from history where people disagree about whether the President overstepped his or her authority. Briefly explain how the President used his or her power. Then comment on whether the amount of power that the President had was appropriate for the circumstances. (*Hint:* Issues of presidential authority often arise in times of war or other national crisis.)

_____

_____

_____

_____

_____

_____

II. Executive Powers

Find Out

A. Review the President's executive powers. Then define them and give an example of each.

Ordinance Power

Definition _____

Example _____

Appointment Power

Definition _____

Example _____

Removal Power

Definition _____

Example _____

What Do You Think?

B. Which of the powers listed above is the most important? Explain.

_____

_____

_____

_____

➔ Find Out

C. Review the case of *U.S.* v. *Nixon* and the Supreme Court's decision in the case. Under what conditions should a President be allowed to claim executive privilege? Explain.

_____

_____

_____

_____

_____

III. Executive, Diplomatic, Military, and Legislative Powers

➔ Find Out

A. Review the roles of the President and his or her powers. Then fill in the chart below.

Roles of the President	Presidential Powers
Chief Executive	*power to execute and enforce federal laws*
Chief Diplomat	
Commander in Chief	
Chief Legislator	

🧑 What Do You Think?

B. Of the powers listed above, which is the most essential? Why?

_____

_____

_____

_____

→ Find Out

C. The Framers placed checks on the President's power. Other limits have developed over time. Using your online or print textbook and your knowledge of government, briefly describe each limit and its effect.

Limits	Effects
Public Opinion	an unpopular President lacks influence; the public can vote the President out of office
International Opinion	
Term Limits	
Party System	
Legislative Checks	
Judicial Checks	
Bureaucracy	

⚫ What Do You Think?

D. Return to the scale of power that you filled in at the beginning of the lesson. With the additional information you have gathered, would you change your rating of where you would place an ideal President on the scale? Explain.

_____

_____

◀ No Real Power | | | | | | | | | Absolute Power ▶

Apply What You've Learned Activity

What do people in your community think about the power of the President? Use this worksheet to answer the Apply What You've Learned questions in your print or online textbook. Interview at least 10 voters (Independent, Republican, and Democratic) in your community. Use the table below to summarize the responses you receive.

Over the past decade, do you think the President overstepped his authority? If so, when?	_____ _____ _____ _____
Over the past decade, do you think the President needed more authority? If so, when?	_____ _____ _____ _____
Over your lifetime, has the power of the President changed? How?	_____ _____ _____ _____

A. With which opinions do you most agree or disagree? Explain.

_____

_____

B. Did your opinions change as a result of the interviews you conducted? Explain.

_____

_____

C. Give two examples of events or situations that could change your opinion.

   1. _____

   2. _____

Essay

How much power should the President have?

In 1789, the new United States government began an experiment in constitutional democracy—with a President at its helm. They looked to the future full of hope and fear. As you read the quotations about the presidency below, consider the concerns of the Framers and the reasons for their fear.

> " The first man at the helm will be a good one. Nobody knows what sort may come afterwards . . . the executive will be increasing here, as elsewhere, till it ends in monarchy.
>
> — *Benjamin Franklin*

> " Make him too weak—the legislature will usurp his power. Make him too strong—he will usurp the legislature.
>
> — *Gouveneur Morris*

What Do You Think?

What is your opinion? Write a response to the Essential Question, **How much power should the President have?** Consider your thoughts on the quotations above, the Guiding Questions in your textbook, and the activities you have done in your Journal. See page 219 for a rubric on writing an Essential Question essay.

Don't Forget

Your answer to this question will help you think about the Unit 4 Essential Question: **What makes a good President?**

CHAPTER 15 Government at Work: The Bureaucracy

Warmup

 Is the bureaucracy essential to good government?

A. From regulations on working an after-school job to the mail that is delivered to your home every day, the activities of the federal bureaucracy affect your life on a daily basis. List five ways in which you come in contact with elements of the federal bureaucracy between the time you wake up in the morning until you leave the house for school.

1. _____
2. _____
3. _____
4. _____
5. _____

B. Using your list above, answer the following questions:

1. Is it possible for you to leave your home without coming into contact with any of these governmental influences? Why or why not?

_____
_____

2. Select one item from your list and describe two benefits and two drawbacks of the government's involvement in that element of your morning routine?

_____
_____
_____
_____

3. Do the benefits of the government's involvement outweigh the drawbacks? Why or why not?

_____
_____
_____

Exploration

I. The Federal Bureaucracy

➔ Find Out

A. Using your print or online textbook or other sources, complete the table below showing the features of a bureaucracy and the benefits of each feature.

Features of a Bureaucracy	Benefits of a Bureaucracy
_____	_____
_____ ➔	_____
_____	_____

B. A bureaucracy's organizational chart is shaped like a pyramid, with more workers at the bottom than at the top. Most organizations are structured in this manner. Choose an organization with which you are familiar, for example, your school, a school club, a sports team, your employer, or your local government. Create an organizational chart for the group you selected. To help you determine where you should place each unit within the hierarchy, keep in mind the following:

- Who is the final decision maker?
- Who manages the organization?
- Who are the main source of labor?

→ Find Out

C. In a complex organization such as the Federal Government, there are many bureaucracies within bureaucracies. Use the chart below to outline a possible structure for the Department of Defense. Choose the various levels from the list below.

- Departments of the Army, Navy, and Air Force
- Secretary of Defense
- President of the United States
- Joint Chiefs of Staff
- Secretaries of the Army, Navy, and Air Force

The Defense Department

👤 What Do You Think?

D. Consider the organizational charts you have created for Parts B and C above. In addition to the benefits of this type of organization listed in Part A, what other benefits of a bureaucracy are illustrated by your charts?

_____

_____

_____

_____

_____

II. Executive Office of the President

→ Find Out

A. Review the various agencies and offices that make up the Executive Office of the President in your print or online textbook or other sources, and then complete the outline.

I. Executive Office of the President

  A. White House Office

    1. <u>Nerve center of the executive branch</u>

    2. <u>Includes the President's inner circle of advisors</u>

    3. <u>Housed in the West Wing of the White House</u>

  B. National Security Council

    1. _____

    2. _____

    3. _____

    4. _____

  C. Office of Management and Budget

    1. _____

    2. _____

    3. _____

    4. _____

B. Use your print or online textbook or other sources to learn the steps involved in creating a budget for the Federal Government. Then complete the flowchart below.

> Federal agencies prepare and submit spending estimates

↓

> _____

↓

> _____

↓

> _____

↓

> _____

↓

> _____

↓

> _____

↓

> OMB monitors spending

What Do You Think?

C. Choose one of the agencies of the Executive Office of the President and explain how the basic features of a bureaucracy are reflected in it.

_____

_____

_____

_____

III. The Executive Departments

Find Out

A. Use your print or online textbook or other sources to find out which three executive departments were established in 1789. List the departments below with a brief description of the work they do.

The First Executive Departments	Description

What Do You Think?

B. Why do you think these three departments were set up before all others? What other important position was created in 1789?

_____

_____

_____

_____

Find Out

C. What factors does the President consider when choosing Cabinet members? Use the web diagram below to list these factors.

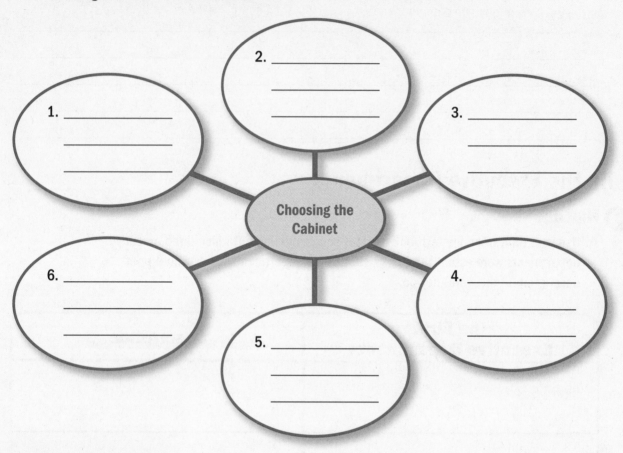

What Do You Think?

D. Which of these factors do you find to be most important? Using the numbers from Part C, place each in the appropriate place on the scale below, then explain your answer on another sheet of paper.

Least Important ← | | | | | | | | → Most Important

What Do You Think?

E. What are two main responsibilities of a Cabinet member? Which do you think is each member's major focus? Why?

_____

_____

_____

IV. Independent Agencies

➔ Find Out

A. Review the various types of independent agencies. Then complete the chart below, filling in information for the types of agencies, their defining characteristics, and some examples of each.

Independent Agencies		
Type	**Defining Characteristics**	**Examples**
independent executive agencies		

B. Use your print or online textbook or other sources to read about the civil service system in the 1800s compared with that system today. Use the following space to describe how the system changed with the passage of the Pendleton Act.

Before

After ↓ **Pendleton Act of 1883**

👤 What Do You Think?

C. The civil service system is part of the executive branch bureaucracy. Do you think this segment of the bureaucracy contributes to good government? Explain your answer.

_____

_____

_____

_____

Apply What You've Learned Activity

What federal agencies are operating in your area? What is the nature of their work? Use this worksheet to answer the Apply What You've Learned questions in your print or online textbook. Interview a federal worker and use the table below to summarize the responses you receive.

What department is responsible for the work of your agency?	_____
In which Cabinet department is your agency located?	_____
Is it one of the larger agencies of that department?	Yes _____ No _____ _____
What are your agency's key responsibilities?	_____ _____
How and by whom are the agency's decisions made?	_____ _____
Do you think the organizational structure of your agency is efficient?	Yes _____ No _____ _____
Could it be improved?	Yes _____ No _____
If so, how?	_____ _____

A. Did anything you learned during the interview surprise you? If so, describe what it was and explain why it was unexpected.

_____

_____

B. Based on your interview, on a separate sheet of paper write a brief summary of how you think the operation of this federal agency could be improved.

Essay

Is the bureaucracy essential to good government?

The federal bureaucracy has gone through a variety of changes since its creation. It has also borne the burden of many jokes and criticisms. However, considering the size of the nation and the expectations of Americans, the Federal Government does accomplish its work. As you review the sources about the federal bureaucracy below, keep in mind the purpose of government.

> **Better the occasional faults of a Government that lives in a spirit of charity than the constant omission of a Government frozen in the ice of its own indifference.**
>
> — *President Franklin Roosevelt, 1936*

> **The nine most terrifying words in the English language are, 'I'm from the government and I'm here to help.'**
>
> — *President Ronald Reagan, 1986*

What Do You Think?

What is your opinion? Write a response to the Essential Question, **Is the bureaucracy essential to good government?** Consider your thoughts on the quotations and political cartoon above, the Guiding Questions in your textbook, and the activities you have done in your Journal. See page 219 for a rubric on writing an Essential Question essay.

Don't Forget

Your answer to this question will help you think about the Unit 4 Essential Question: **What makes a good President?**

CHAPTER

16 Financing Government

Warmup

How should the federal budget reflect Americans' priorities?

A. Suppose you lived on your own without the financial support of your parent(s) or guardian(s). You would have to find employment and then budget the money you earned. Consider the categories below. Cross off any that do not apply and add any that are not shown. Then use the blanks to the right to assign a percentage to each category. For example, would you spend 20 percent of your salary on food? What about clothing? (*Remember:* Your total percentage cannot exceed 100 percent.)

My Budget

Food _____   Internet service _____

Clothing _____   Cell phone _____

Heat _____   Recreation _____

Electricity _____   Other:

Telephone _____   _____

Cable/satellite TV _____ _____

Vehicle payment/car
insurance/gas _____

B. Use your percentages to complete the circle graph above showing the percentage of your total earnings spent in each category.

1. Describe how these percentages reflect your personal priorities.

_____

_____

2. Look at your circle graph. Of those categories with smaller percentages, which would you give up so that you could afford your highest priorities? Explain.

_____

_____

CHAPTER 16 How should the federal budget reflect
Americans' priorities?

Name: _____

Exploration

I. The Federal Government's Income

→ Find Out

A. The Constitution is very clear about the limitations on the taxing power. Using your print
or online textbook or other sources, complete the web to outline those limitations.

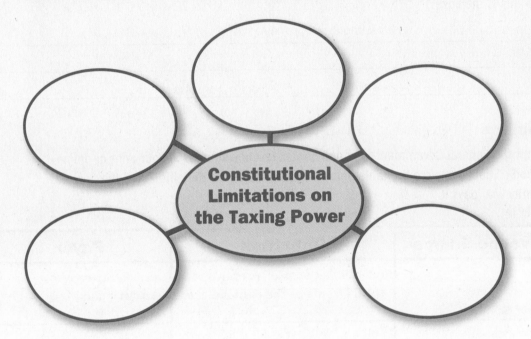

Constitutional
Limitations on
the Taxing Power

Why do you think the Framers included these limitations on the power to tax? Do you
think they are necessary?

_____

_____

_____

B. Read Article I, Section 8, Clause 1 of the Constitution. List the three reasons why Congress
is given the taxing power. Then, using the number of each reason, categorize each of the
outlays listed on the next page under each reason.

1. _____

2. _____

3. _____

CHAPTER 16 How should the federal budget reflect Americans' priorities?

Name: _____

_____ a. Purchasing of missiles	_____ e. Military officers' salaries
_____ b. Space exploration	_____ f. Federal judges' salaries
_____ c. Coining money	___1___ g. Paying interest on the public debt
_____ d. Providing social service programs	

👤 What Do You Think?

C. Which category above seems to cover the largest share of federal spending? Why do you think this is the case?

_____

_____

_____

⮕ Find Out

D. Review the Federal Government's tax and nontax revenue sources in your print or online textbook. Then, complete the table below with the source, its definition, and the person or entity who pays it.

Revenue Source	Definition	Payer
Income tax	A tax levied on each person's total income of the previous year	all Americans who receive income

CHAPTER 16 How should the federal budget reflect
Americans' priorities?

Name: _____

What Do You Think?

E. According to the chart on the previous page, who provides most of the Federal
Government's funding? Taking this into consideration, how much input should this
source have on how and on what the government spends its revenue? Explain.

_____

_____

_____

II. Spending and the Budget

Find Out

A. Federal Government spending can be described as either *controllable* or *uncontrollable.*
Review these terms in your print or online textbook. Then determine whether each example in
the chart below is a controllable or an uncontrollable expense, and indicate whether you think
the American public would consider these examples a low, medium, or high priority.

Example	Controllable or Uncontrollable	Priority Level
Pollution Control		
Food Stamps		
Space Exploration		
Social Security		
Agricultural Research		
Military Development		
Veterans' Benefits		
Interest on the Public Debt		
Energy Conservation		
Homeland Security		

B. Circle the expense that you consider to be the highest American priority. Is this your highest
priority? If yes, explain why you place this category at such a level. If not, what is your
highest priority? (*Note:* Your highest priority does not need to come from the list above.)

_____

_____

CHAPTER 16 How should the federal budget reflect
Americans' priorities?

Name: _____

C. Review how the Federal Government creates its annual budget in your print or online
textbook or other sources. Then complete the chart below with the responsibilities of the
President, the OMB, and Congress.

President	Office of Management and Budget (OMB)	Congress
	• Reviews each federal agency's proposed spending plan	

What Do You Think?

D. Does the American public have any influence on the federal budget? Choose one of the steps
in the budget creation process above and describe how it includes the public's involvement.

_____

_____

III. Borrowing and the Public Debt

Find Out

A. Review the reasons for the Federal Government's need to borrow money in your print or
online textbook or other sources and list them below.

1. _____

2. _____

B. Review the process of federal borrowing. Then answer the questions that follow.

1. Who must authorize government borrowing? _____

2. What department is responsible for government borrowing? _____

3. How does the government acquire borrowed funds? _____

_____

4. What occurs when the government borrows money? _____

_____

Name: _____

What Do You Think?

C. Many Americans are concerned with the increasing public debt. Do you think their concerns are valid?

_____

_____

What three ways would you suggest to address the problem?

1. _____

2. _____

3. _____

IV. Fiscal and Monetary Policy

Find Out

A. Review the fiscal policy options available to the Federal Government in your print or online textbook or other sources. Describe each below and then indicate what is expected to occur when each option is increased or decreased.

1. _____

   Increase _____

   Decrease _____

2. _____

   Increase _____

   Decrease _____

What Do You Think?

B. The use of monetary and fiscal policy allows the Federal Government to influence the nation's economy. Some Americans criticize the government's involvement in the economy, while others think it is necessary.

1. Cite one advantage and one disadvantage of the government's ability to influence the economy.

   Advantage _____

   Disadvantage _____

2. Do you think the government should be responsible for the stability of the nation's economy? Explain.

_____

_____

_____

Name: _____

Apply What You've Learned Activity

What issues do most Americans think should be the government's priorities? Use this worksheet to help with the Apply What You've Learned activity in your print or online textbook. Take a poll of 10 to 15 individuals in your community, and use the table below to summarize the results of your poll.

Priorities	Poll Results
What issues are priorities to Americans today?	
Which one do you think is of the utmost importance to most Americans?	
Which one is the most important to you?	
Actions	**Poll Results**
Within the last six months, has the Federal Government taken any action to address that issue? If so, what?	
Which, if any, federal programs or services do you think could be cut back or abolished to help deal with the issue?	
If none, would you be willing to pay additional taxes to cover the cost of a new program?	
If not, how should the government pay for it?	
Evaluations	**Poll Results**
Do you think the Federal Government is responsive to the priorities of Americans? Why or why not?	

A. Do you agree with those you polled on their choice of the highest priority? Explain.

_____

_____

B. Which responses provided new insight on American priorities that affected your opinion on government spending? Explain.

_____

_____

CHAPTER 16 How should the federal budget reflect
Americans' priorities?

Name: _____

Essay

How should the federal budget reflect Americans' priorities?

For the Federal Government to provide the services necessary for the well-being of the nation, it requires a large amount of revenue. At times, the government must borrow heavily to provide these services. As you read the quotations about financing government below, consider the expectations of the American public and their concerns about the national debt.

> The constitutional purpose of a budget is to make government responsive to public opinion and responsible for its acts.
>
> — *William Howard Taft*

> A national debt, if it is not excessive, will be to us a national blessing.
>
> — *Alexander Hamilton, Letter to Robert Morris, April 30, 1781*

> If the Nation is living within its income, its credit is good. If, in some crises, it lives beyond its income for a year or two, it can usually borrow temporarily at reasonable rates. But if . . . it throws discretion to the winds . . . [and] it extends its taxing to the limit of the people's power to pay and continues to pile up deficits, then it is on the road to bankruptcy.
>
> — *Franklin Delano Roosevelt, presidential campaign speech, 1932*

What Do You Think?

What is your opinion? Write a response to the Essential Question, **How should the federal budget reflect Americans' priorities?** Consider your thoughts on the quotations above, the Guiding Questions in your textbook, and the activities you have done in your Journal. See page 219 for a rubric on writing an Essential Question essay.

Don't Forget
Your answer to this question will help you think about the Unit 4 Essential Question:
What makes a good President?

17 Foreign Policy and National Defense

CHAPTER

Warmup

 How should the United States interact with other countries?

A. When should the United States involve itself in international affairs? Review the scenarios below and check Yes or No when you think the event requires American involvement. Then indicate how you think the United States should respond to each event.

Scenario	Yes	No	Type(s) of Response
1. An earthquake hits a large and remote area in central China causing extensive destruction.	___	___	_____
2. A civil war, entering its tenth year between an American-recognized government and a religious separatist group, is threatening to expand into a neighboring country.	___	___	_____
3. A bomb threat is made at the U.S. embassy in Moscow.	___	___	_____
4. Brazilian scientists have determined that a production plant along the Amazon is illegally dumping chemicals into the river.	___	___	_____
5. Citizens of an African country are voting in their first democratic election.	___	___	_____

B. Select one of the scenarios above to which you answered as needing a response by the United States. Why do you think it is important for the United States to take action in this scenario?

_____

_____

_____

_____

_____

Name: _____

Exploration

I. Foreign Policy and Diplomacy

➡ Find Out

A. The way in which the United States interacts with foreign countries has changed dramatically since the republic was created. Summarize each overarching policy below.

Isolationism

_____

_____

Internationalism

_____

_____

B. Review the U.S. foreign policies that have developed since the republic was established. Summarize each policy below and provide either a historic or current example of the use of each.

Monroe Doctrine

Summary _____

Example _____

Deterrence

Summary _____

Example _____

Truman Doctrine

Summary _____

Example _____

Containment

Summary _____

Example _____

Détente

Summary _____

Example _____

Collective Security

Summary _____

Example _____

CHAPTER 17 How should the United States interact with other countries?

Name: _____

➡ Find Out

C. The State Department is the key player in the implementation of foreign policy. Use your print or online textbook to help you list the goals of the State Department. Then provide two real-world examples of each in the concept web below.

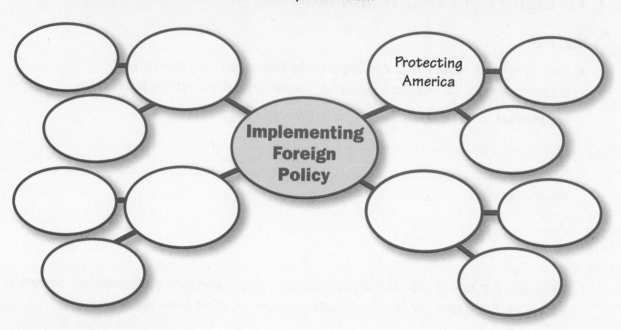

👤 What Do You Think?

D. United States foreign policy has often alternated between isolationism and internationalism. Which policy is now the primary focus of American foreign policy and how do the actions of the United States today illustrate that focus? Explain your reasoning using examples from current events.

_____

_____

_____

_____

II. National Security

➡ Find Out

A. Civilian control of the military is a major principle in the U.S. Constitution. Use your print or online textbook or other sources to research the topic. Then summarize the principle and explain whether you think the issue is still a concern today.

_____

_____

_____

CHAPTER 17 How should the United States interact with other countries?

Name: _____

B. Review the material on the Defense Department in your print or online textbook. Then complete the chart by listing the main responsibilities of each office or department.

The Defense Department	
Office or Department	**Responsibilities**
Secretary of Defense	
Joint Chiefs of Staff	
Department of the Army	
Department of the Navy	
Department of the Air Force	

C. National security is of vital importance to maintaining the well-being of the United States and its citizens. Write a brief description of how the following agencies ensure the nation's security.

Office of the Director of National Intelligence

_____

_____

_____

Department of Homeland Security

_____

_____

_____

👤 What Do You Think?

D. How might the officials and agencies responsible for the national defense and security affect interactions between the United States and other countries?

_____

_____

_____

CHAPTER 17 How should the United States interact
with other countries?

Name: _____

III. Foreign Aid and Alliances

→ Find Out

A. Review the material on foreign aid in your print or online textbook and write the definition
of the term in the space below.

_____

B. If American aid is provided to a foreign country, how does the United States benefit from
providing it?

_____

_____

_____

_____

C. The United States has become a member of several regional security alliances over
the years. Use your print or online textbook or other sources to fill in the chart with five
major alliances, their purposes, and their members.

Regional Security Alliances		
Name	**Purpose**	**Member Nations**
North Atlantic Treaty Organization (NATO)		

Name: _____

→ Find Out

D. The United Nations was created following World War II. According to its charter, what are the organization's main purposes?

1. _____

2. _____

3. _____

E. Using your print or online textbook or other sources, review the six main units of the United Nations. Then describe how the main purposes of the UN are reflected in their responsibilities and activities?

General Assembly _____

_____

Security Council _____

_____

Economic and Social Council _____

_____

Trusteeship Council _____

_____

International Court of Justice _____

_____

Secretariat _____

_____

🙂 What Do You Think?

F. The United States is the wealthiest and most powerful nation in the world. Because of this status, the United States has the ability to help other nations. On the other hand, some nations feel that the United States has too much influence. Considering its foreign aid policy, alliances, and membership in the UN, do you think the United States has too much influence in the affairs of other countries? Why or why not?

_____

_____

_____

_____

_____

_____

Name: _____

Apply What You've Learned Activity

How has the United States provided foreign aid in recent years? Use this worksheet to answer the Apply What You've Learned questions in your print or online textbook. Conduct research on American foreign aid provided to a specific region or country. Use the space below to take notes on your research.

What event led to U.S. involvement?	
For how long did the United States provide support?	
Was American support military or humanitarian in nature?	
Did the type of support change over time? If so, how?	
Were other organizations involved? Which ones?	
What were the results of American support?	

A. Which cause or event do you think had the most impact on providing American foreign aid?

_____

_____

B. Is the aid program still in effect? If so, are the aims of the foreign aid being met? If not, why not?

_____

_____

C. On a separate sheet of paper, list three benefits this aid is providing to the receiving country and three benefits the United States acquires through providing this aid.

CHAPTER 17 How should the United States interact
with other countries?

Name: _____

Essay

How should the United States interact with other countries?

Unlike the world of 200 years ago, most nations today can no longer avoid interacting with other nations. This is especially true of the United States, to whom many countries look for guidance and support. As you review the quotations about international relations below, consider how peace in the world today depends on international cooperation.

> " There is no security for any of us unless there is security for all.
>
> — *Howard Koch, American screenwriter*

> " I am . . . willing to make it clear that American foreign policy must uphold the sanctity of international treaties. That is the cornerstone on which all relations between nations must rest.
>
> — *Franklin D. Roosevelt, 1933*

> " Since wars begin in the minds of men, it is in the minds of men that the defenses of peace must be constructed.
>
> — *Constitution of the United Nations Educational, Scientific, and Cultural Organization, 1945*

> " The heroes of the world community are not those who withdraw when difficulties ensue, not those who can envision neither the prospect of success nor the consequence of failure—but those who stand the heat of battle, the fight for world peace through the United Nations.
>
> — *Hubert Humphrey, speech, November 17, 1965, New York City*

What Do You Think?

What is your opinion? Write a response to the Essential Question, **How should the United States interact with other countries?** Consider your thoughts on the quotations above, the Guiding Questions in your textbook, and the activities you have done in your Journal. See page 219 for a rubric on writing an Essential Question essay.

Don't Forget

Your answer to this question will help you think about the Unit 4 Essential Question: **What makes a good President?**

UNIT 4 The Executive Branch

Essay Warmup

Examine the following perspectives on the presidency. The questions that follow each perspective will help you focus your thinking on the Unit 4 Essential Question, **What makes a good President?**

> " . . . [R]esearch indicate[s] that great presidents, besides being stubborn and disagreeable, are more extraverted, open to experience, assertive, achievement striving, excitement seeking and more open to fantasy, aesthetics, feelings, actions, ideas and values. Historically great presidents were low on straightforwardness, vulnerability and order.
>
> — *American Psychological Association News Release announcing the results of a study of the personalities of the Presidents, August 2000*

1. What are the qualities of great Presidents, according to the study above?

_____

_____

2. Choose a President you consider great. Do you think this President possessed the qualities described above? Explain.

_____

_____

> " All our great presidents were leaders of thought at times when certain ideas in the life of the nation had to be clarified.
>
> — *Franklin D. Roosevelt*

3. Give an example of a President you would consider a "leader of thought" and explain your choice.

_____

_____

_____

_____

In a pun on the names of cars and Presidents, Gerald Ford was known during his presidency as "a Ford, not a Lincoln."

4. Study the cartoon and answer the following questions:

a. What does the car represent? _____

b. Why is the flag at half-mast? _____

c. Why does the cartoonist include a child in the cartoon? _____

_____

5. What does the cartoon suggest about Ford's presidency?

_____

_____

_____

_____

_____

👤 What Do You Think?

6. Choose one of the documents above and explain how it helps you answer the Unit 4 Essential Question, **What makes a good President?**

_____

_____

_____

_____

_____

_____

UNIT 4 The Executive Branch

Essay

What makes a good President?

Write an essay that answers the Essential Question, **What makes a good President?** Use your answers to the Essential Question warmup questions on the previous pages, your answers to the chapter Essential Questions, and what you have learned in this unit. Keep in mind that your essay should reflect your thoughtful and well-supported personal point of view. Answering the prompts below will help you structure your essay. Go to page 219 for a rubric for writing an Essential Question essay.

Thesis Statement: _____

_____

Body Paragraph 1	Body Paragraph 2	Body Paragraph 3
Main Idea	**Main Idea**	**Main Idea**
_____	_____	_____
_____	_____	_____
_____	_____	_____
_____	_____	_____
Supporting Details	**Supporting Details**	**Supporting Details**
1. _____	1. _____	1. _____
_____	_____	_____
_____	_____	_____
2. _____	2. _____	2. _____
_____	_____	_____
_____	_____	_____
3. _____	3. _____	3. _____
_____	_____	_____
_____	_____	_____

Conclusion: _____

_____

Unit 5

The Judicial Branch

UNIT 5 The Judicial Branch

The U.S. Supreme Court

Warmup

What should be the role of the judicial branch?

"Equal Justice Under Law" are the words carved into the U.S. Supreme Court building in Washington, D.C. The decisions made by this Court and other courts in the judicial branch affect almost every aspect of your life. In Unit 5, you will study the federal court system and explore possible answers to the Essential Question above.

A. There has been much debate over the role of the courts and responsibilities of judges. Read the pairs of statements below. Check one statement in each pair that you agree with the most.

____ A court's decision should be final.
____ An allowance must be made for some court decisions to be appealed to a higher court.

____ Judges should interpret laws according to the needs of society at the time.
____ Judges should interpret laws only according to the Framers' intentions in writing the Constitution.

____ Judges should be elected by popular vote and serve a limited term.
____ Judges should be appointed and serve for life.

____ Judges should focus on individual rights.
____ Judges should focus on the common good of society.

____ Judges should be absolutely neutral.
____ Judges should be allowed to incorporate their judicial and political philosophy into their decisions.

B. Consider why we need a court system. Explain what you think society would be like without a way to address injustices.

_____

_____

_____

_____

_____

_____

CHAPTER 18 The Federal Court System

Warmup

Does the structure of the federal court system allow it to administer justice effectively?

What does "administer justice effectively" mean to you? Complete the statements below with words or phrases that describe "justice" in your view. Some examples have been provided.

Judges should	• _____ • _____ • _____
Laws should	• _____ • _____ • *be consistent.*
Trials should	• _____ • _____ • _____
Members of a jury should	• _____ • _____ • *be impartial.*
Someone charged with a crime or civil suit should	• _____ • _____ • *be tried in a timely manner.*
Cases that reach the Supreme Court should	• _____ • _____ • *involve significant points of law.*

CHAPTER 18 Does the structure of the federal court system allow it to administer justice effectively?

Name: _____

Exploration

I. Article III and Article I Courts

→ Find Out

A. Read Article III, Section 1 and Article I, Section 8, Clause 9 of the Constitution. What does each part state?

1. _____

_____

2. _____

_____

B. Find examples of the Article III and Article I courts in your print or online textbook. List the examples below in the appropriate column, and then answer the questions that follow.

Article III Courts	Article I Courts
(also called _____ courts)	(also called _____ courts)
•	•
•	•
•	•
•	•
	•
	•

1. Which is the only court mentioned in the Constitution? _____

2. What are the two levels of federal courts? _____

3. How are the inferior courts further divided? _____

4. Which type of inferior courts did Congress create? _____

CHAPTER 18 Does the structure of the federal court system allow it to administer justice effectively?

Name: _____

What Do You Think?

C. Why do you think there are so many types of courts in the federal court system?

_____

_____

_____

II. Federal Court Jurisdiction

Find Out

A. Review the jurisdiction of federal courts in your print or online textbook. Then fill in the information on both sides of the T-chart below.

Federal Court Jurisdiction

Exclusive jurisdiction *Definition:*	**Subject matter** a case that involves an issue in the Constitution; a federal law, treaty, or act of Congress; maritime law; an official of a foreign government; a person charged with a federal crime; patent or copyright issues **Parties involved**
Concurrent jurisdiction *Definition:*	**Types of cases**
Original jurisdiction *Definition:*	**Which federal courts have this jurisdiction?** District courts, the Supreme Court, U.S. Court of International Trade, U.S. Court of Federal Claims, U.S. Tax Court, Territorial Courts, Courts of the District of Columbia
Appellate jurisdiction *Definition:*	**Which federal courts have this jurisdiction?**

CHAPTER 18 Does the structure of the federal court system
allow it to administer justice effectively?

Name: _____

What Do You Think?

B. In the T-chart, you described the jurisdiction of federal courts. What kinds of cases do
you think would be heard in *State* and *local* courts?

_____

_____

_____

_____

III. Structure and Functions of Inferior Courts

Find Out

A. Review the jurisdiction and functions of the inferior courts. Then complete the chart below.

Name of Court	Jurisdiction/Functions
District Courts Number: _____	
Courts of Appeals Number: _____	
Court of Appeals for the Federal Circuit	
U.S. Court of International Trade	
Court of Appeals for the Armed Forces	appellate jurisdiction over court-martial convictions
Court of Appeals for Veterans Claims	
Court of Federal Claims	
Territorial Courts	hear cases in the Virgin Islands, Guam, and the Northern Mariana Islands
District of Columbia Courts	
U.S. Tax Court	

CHAPTER 18 Does the structure of the federal court system
allow it to administer justice effectively?

Name: _____

B. Review the appellate path of federal inferior courts in your print or online textbook.
Then use the information to answer the questions below.

CASE 1: A citizen is accused of counterfeiting.

In what type of court does the case begin? _____

If the case is appealed, where would it go next? _____

CASE 2: An American importer of fish claims that the U.S. Department of Commerce
placed an unusually high tax on fish fillets from Vietnam.

Where does this case begin? _____

The American importer loses and appeals to which court? _____

CASE 3: An Ohio company claims that a Florida company produced an identical product,
and files for copyright violation.

Where does the case begin? _____

The Ohio company loses and appeals to which court? _____

CASE 4: A citizen in Guam is accused of kidnapping.

Where does the case begin? _____

The defendant is found guilty and appeals. Where does the case go? _____

CASE 5: A citizen claims that the U.S. Forest Service harmed his crops by damming a
stream upriver on government land, and he sues for damages.

Where does this case begin? _____

The citizen loses and appeals to which court? _____

CASE 6: The Nuclear Regulatory Commission appeals a case.

Where is the appeal heard? _____

👤 What Do You Think?

C. Invent two new inferior courts with narrowly defined jurisdiction. Explain how they would
help the federal courts more effectively administer justice.

1. _____

_____

2. _____

_____

CHAPTER 18 Does the structure of the federal court system allow it to administer justice effectively?

Name: _____

IV. Structure and Functions of the Supreme Court

➔ Find Out

A. Review information about the Supreme Court in your print or online textbook. Then answer the questions below.

1. Over what cases does the Supreme Court have exclusive and original jurisdiction?

controversies involving two or more States; cases against ambassadors or other

public ministers

2. Which jurisdiction does the Supreme Court utilize the most, by far? _____

3. About how many cases does the Court hear each year? _____

4. What happens after the Court agrees to hear a case?

_____

_____

B. Use your print or online textbook to fill in the diagram below.

How a Case Reaches the Supreme Court

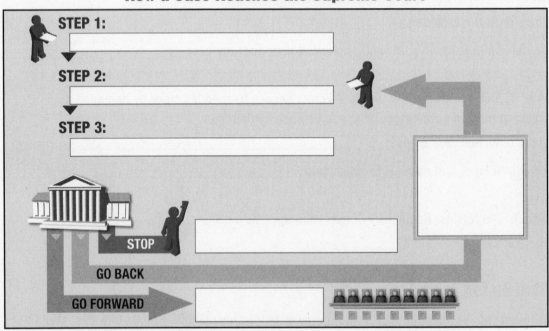

STEP 1:

STEP 2:

STEP 3:

STOP

GO BACK

GO FORWARD

👤 What Do You Think?

C. Why do you think the path of appeal to the Supreme Court involves so many steps?

_____

_____

CHAPTER 18 Does the structure of the federal court system allow it to administer justice effectively?

Name: _____

Apply What You've Learned Activity

Interview a federal judge or lawyer who has experience with federal cases. Use this worksheet to write his or her answers to the Apply What You've Learned questions from your print or online textbook.

Questions	Responses
What do you think is the purpose of the law?	
What is the role of the courts in our system of government?	
What do you think are the advantages of trying a case in federal court, as compared to a State or local court? The disadvantages?	

A. Based on the interview you conducted and the content you have learned in this chapter, has your opinion about the federal court system changed in any way? Explain your answer.

_____

_____

_____

B. Make a list of at least five qualifications you think the President should consider in selecting a justice for the Supreme Court or any federal judge.

1. _____

2. _____

3. _____

4. _____

5. _____

Explain your qualifications.

_____

_____

CHAPTER 18 Does the structure of the federal court system
allow it to administer justice effectively?

Name: _____

Essay

Does the structure of the federal court system allow it to administer justice effectively?

Most of the cases the Supreme Court agrees to hear today involve constitutional issues. Before the Judiciary Act of 1925, however, *anyone* had the right to appeal to the Supreme Court if a case involved more than $1,000 or a conviction of a capital crime. In addition, before 1891 Supreme Court justices rode circuit, or traveled around a large region to hear cases. The federal court system was restructured to reduce the number of cases heard by the Supreme Court.

> Some justices were forced to ride hundreds of miles each year in trains and horse-drawn coaches over poorly kept roads. In 1839, for example, the nine justices traveled nearly 30,000 miles riding circuit. Justice Stephen J. Field's Pacific circuit took him by sail to the West Coast, traveling by rail across Panama. After the completion of the transcontinental railroad in 1869, he at least was able to make the journey by rail. . . . The 1890s and the new century witnessed a spurt in regulatory legislation at the state and federal levels, and the Court's docket once again exploded. It grew from 723 cases in 1900 to 1,116 in 1910.
>
> — *History of the Supreme Court, www.historyofsupremecourt.org/overview.htm*

What Do You Think?

What is your opinion? Write a response to the Essential Question, **Does the structure of the federal court system allow it to administer justice effectively?** Consider your thoughts on the quotation above, the Guiding Questions in your textbook, and the activities you have completed in your Journal. See page 219 for a rubric on writing an Essential Question essay.

Don't Forget

Your answer to this question will help you think about the Unit 5 Essential Question: **What should be the role of the judicial branch?**

Warmup

How can the judiciary balance individual rights with the common good?

A. What does the phrase *common good* mean to you?

_____

_____

B. Which do you think is more important—protecting individual rights or protecting the common good? Explain your answer.

_____

_____

_____

C. Individual freedoms of religion, speech, press, and assembly are not absolute. They can be restricted when they infringe upon the rights of others, violate laws, or threaten safety. Read the statements below, which describe restrictions on or support for individual freedoms. Write whether you think each statement is true (T) or false (F).

_____ **1.** Public officials may prevent the publication of articles insulting to them.

_____ **2.** Worshipers may use poisonous snakes in religious rituals.

_____ **3.** Religious groups do not have to salute the flag.

_____ **4.** No Internet site may knowingly transmit indecent speech or images to any person under age 18.

_____ **5.** Animals may be sacrificed in church services.

_____ **6.** A permit is required to hold a religious parade on public property.

_____ **7.** Government has the right to prevent publication of material that it says is harmful to national security.

_____ **8.** Government can draft those who have religious objections to military service.

_____ **9.** Reporters are constitutionally protected against having to reveal their sources during a trial.

_____ **10.** Government officials may prohibit a group with racist ideas from holding a demonstration in public.

_____ **11.** It is legal to read aloud a prayer before public high school graduation ceremonies.

_____ **12.** It is legal to display a Christmas tree in a government building.

CHAPTER 19 How can the judiciary balance individual rights with the common good?

Name: _____

Exploration

I. The Unalienable Rights

→ Find Out

A. Use your print or online textbook to define or describe the following:

1. civil liberties: _____

_____

2. civil rights: _____

_____

3. Bill of Rights: _____

_____

4. unalienable rights: _____

_____

5. 14th Amendment's Due Process Clause: _____

_____

6. 9th Amendment: _____

_____

_____

B. Complete the diagram below by listing the 1st Amendment freedoms and rights.

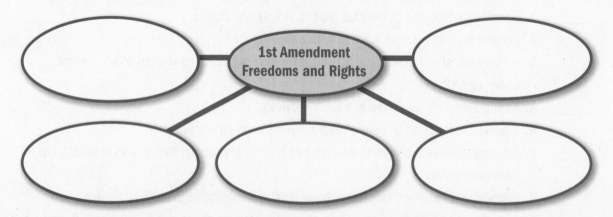

1st Amendment Freedoms and Rights

C. Explain what this statement means: Rights are relative, not absolute.

_____

_____

_____

CHAPTER 19 How can the judiciary balance individual rights with the common good?

Name: _____

D. Explain how civil liberties conflict with the common good in the following scenarios:

1. A public demonstration blocks traffic for hours.

Civil liberty: _____

Common good: _____

2. A neighbor blares her stereo in the middle of the night.

Civil liberty: _____

Common good: _____

3. The government halts publication of war-related information.

Civil liberty: _____

Common good: _freedom of the press and the public's right to know_

What Do You Think?

E. What additional rights would you consider "unalienable"? Explain.

_____

_____

_____

II. Government and Religion

Find Out

A. The constitutional guarantee of religious freedom has two parts: the Establishment Clause and the Free Exercise Clause. Use your print or online textbook to find the answers to the questions about these two clauses below.

Establishment Clause
1. What does it create?
2. What does it prohibit?

Free Exercise Clause
1. What does it guarantee?
2. What does it NOT protect?

CHAPTER 19 How can the judiciary balance individual rights
with the common good?

Name: _____

B. Use your print or online textbook to review the religious actions in public schools that
have been found unconstitutional by the Supreme Court. List five examples below, and
write the reason behind the Court's decisions.

1. Action: _____

_____

2. Action: _____

_____

3. Action: _____

_____

4. Action: _____

_____

5. Action: _____

_____

Reason for Court's decisions: _____

_____

_____

What religious actions are allowed in public schools? List three examples below.

6. Action: _Individuals can pray when and as they choose in any place._____

7. Action: _____

8. Action: _____

C. Use your print or online textbook to review the three standards of the *Lemon* test, which is
used to determine whether a State law amounts to an "establishment" of religion. Write
these standards in the diagram below.

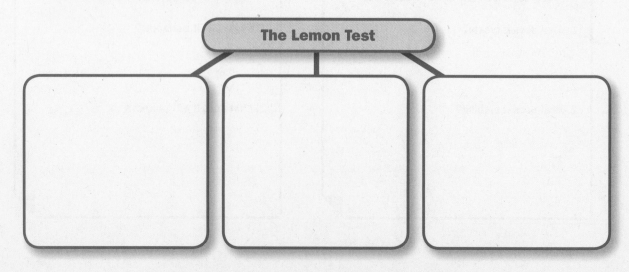

The Lemon Test

CHAPTER 19 How can the judiciary balance individual rights with the common good?

Name: _____

D. Why has the Court ruled that the following actions violate the Establishment Clause?

1. Seasonal displays of a single religious doctrine at government buildings

_____

_____

_____

2. Public displays of the Ten Commandments inside government buildings

_____

_____

_____

E. Review the Free Exercise Clause. Give four examples of government regulations that have limited the free exercise of religion in order to benefit the common good.

Law upheld: _vaccination of school children, even if their religion opposes it_

Law upheld: _____

Law upheld: _____

Law upheld: _____

F. Give three examples of laws that the Court has overturned in order to uphold the free exercise of religion.

Law overturned: _____

Law overturned: _____

Law overturned: _____

👤 What Do You Think?

G. How are individual rights balanced with the common good when religious expression is prohibited in public schools?

_____

_____

_____

_____

_____

_____

CHAPTER 19 How can the judiciary balance individual rights with the common good?

Name: _____

III. Freedom of Expression

➔ Find Out

A. The 1st and 14th amendment guarantees of free speech and press protect a person's right to speak freely and to hear what others have to say. Some forms of expression are not protected, however. Review the types of expression and their restrictions in your print or online textbook. Then complete the chart below.

Type of Expression	Restrictions
Seditious speech *Definition:*	
Obscenity *Definition:*	
Symbolic speech *Definition:*	
Commercial speech *Definition:*	

B. Complete the diagram below. Identify at least three cases, issues, or examples that protect freedom of the press, and at least three exceptions that allow prior restraint on publications.

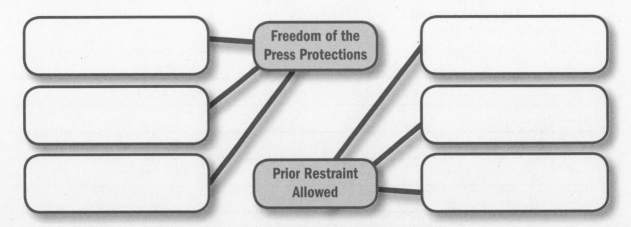

Name: _____

What Do You Think?

C. The Supreme Court and lower courts have ruled that students' freedoms of speech and press are limited by the "special characteristics of the school environment."

1. What might these "special characteristics" be?

_____

_____

2. Does limiting individual rights of students benefit the common good of the school? Explain.

_____

_____

IV. The Right to Assemble

Find Out

A. (1) What are some examples of assembly? (2) What are the advantages of joining a group to protest a policy or to express an opinion?

_____

_____

_____

B. The government may place reasonable limits on when, where, and how an assembly may be conducted. List four examples of these "time-place-manner" rules applied to organized demonstrations to keep the public peace.

Example 1: _____

Example 2: _____

Example 3: _____

Example 4: _____

C. Review *Forsyth County* v. *Nationalist Movement*, 1992, in your print or online textbook. What issue did this case decide regarding government's rules about assembly?

_____

_____

What Do You Think?

D. What might happen if Americans were not allowed to protest?

_____

_____

CHAPTER 19 How can the judiciary balance individual rights with the common good?

Name: _____

Apply What You've Learned Activity

A. Suppose you are helping to organize a demonstration for a political cause. Write three questions you should ask to determine if the Supreme Court would consider your demonstration to be constitutionally protected. Use this worksheet to write your questions and possible answers.

Question	Possible Answer

B. Now create an outline of information that you would include in a brochure for the participants in your demonstration under two headings: "Know Your Rights" and "Know Your Limits." In the space below, list or illustrate the rights and limits on freedom of speech, press, and assembly.

Know Your Rights	Know Your Limits

CHAPTER 19 How can the judiciary balance individual rights with the common good?

Name: _____

Essay

How can the judiciary balance individual rights with the common good?

Since America's earliest days as a nation, public and judicial opinion has been divided over the extent of 1st Amendment freedoms. Some people believe the Supreme Court has gone too far in ruling for the common good or for individual rights. Others believe the Court has not gone far enough.

> [I]f there is any principle of the Constitution that more imperatively calls for attachment than any other it is the principle of free thought—not free thought for those who agree with us but freedom for the thought that we hate.
>
> — *Justice Oliver Wendell Holmes,* United States *v.* Schwimmer

What Do You Think?

What is your opinion? Write a response to the Essential Question, **How can the judiciary balance individual rights with the common good?** Consider your thoughts on the information above, the Guiding Questions in your textbook, and the activities you have done in your Journal. See page 219 for a rubric on writing an Essential Question essay.

Don't Forget

Your answer to this question will help you think about the Unit 5 Essential Question: **What should be the role of the judicial branch?**

Name: _____

20 Civil Liberties: Protecting Individual Rights

Warmup

To what extent has the judiciary protected the rights of privacy, security, and personal freedom?

To protect citizens' rights of privacy, security, and personal freedom, the courts require that laws be fair. For each action below, write the law that you think has been broken. Then state whether you believe that law is fair, and why or why not.

Action	Law Broken	Is the law fair? Why or why not?	To whom does the law apply?
1. A student skips school.	Law against truancy; compulsory education law		students
2. A person drives while under the influence of alcohol.			
3. A factory dumps industrial waste into a local river.			
4. Police enter your home without a search warrant.			
5. The police arrest you on suspicion of a criminal act. You are held in jail for five days without being told what crime you are accused of committing.			

CHAPTER 20 To what extent has the judiciary protected the rights of privacy, security, and personal freedom?

Name: _____

Exploration

I. Due Process of Law

→ Find Out

A. Due process requires government and law enforcement to act fairly and according to established rules. Review the 5th Amendment and Section 1 of the 14th Amendment in your print or online textbook.

1. What limit does the 5th Amendment place on government?

_____

_____

2. What limit does Section 1 of the 14th Amendment place on government?

_____

_____

_____

😀 What Do You Think?

B. Why is it important that laws not only be fair but also consistent across all situations and classes of people?

_____

_____

_____

II. The Right of Privacy

→ Find Out

A. The right of privacy is not specifically mentioned in the Constitution. However, the guarantees of due process create a right of privacy. Review the case of *Stanley* v. *Georgia,* 1969, in your print or online textbook. What important issue did this case decide regarding the right of privacy?

_____

_____

_____

_____

B. The issues in the chart below concern the right of privacy. Review these issues in your print or online textbook, and explain how the Supreme Court has ruled on them.

Issue	Ruling
1. Possession of obscene materials in one's own home	
2. Use of birth control devices	
3. Right to an abortion	
4. Bugging a public phone booth	
5. Random drug testing of students	

C. What privacy concerns have been raised by the USA Patriot Act?

_____

_____

👤 What Do You Think?

D. Should schools be allowed to conduct "suspicionless" drug tests? Why or why not?

_____

_____

III. Protection of Personal Freedom

➡ Find Out

A. Many of the judiciary's restrictions on government are intended to protect the right of personal freedom.

1. Which amendment outlawed slavery in the United States?

_____

2. Are any forms of involuntary servitude still permitted today? Explain.

_____

_____

CHAPTER 20 To what extent has the judiciary protected the rights of privacy, security, and personal freedom?

Name: _____

B. Review the case of *Jones* v. *Mayer*, 1968, in your print or online textbook. What important issue did this case decide regarding racial discrimination?

_____

_____

👤 What Do You Think?

C. Do you think a person should be forced to work for another to pay off a debt? Why or why not?

_____

_____

IV. Security of Home and Person

➡️ Find Out

A. The 4th Amendment protects people from arbitrary searches and seizures. How does the requirement to show probable cause limit police in search and seizure actions? What is an unreasonable search and seizure?

_____

_____

_____

B. For each situation in the table, indicate whether a search warrant is needed.

Situation	Search warrant needed?
1. When police are acting on an anonymous tip	
2. When evidence is in plain view	
3. When evidence is gained during an informational roadblock	
4. Before searching a vehicle when there is probable cause that it holds evidence of a crime	
5. Before using a dog to sniff around a car for narcotics during a traffic stop	

C. The exclusionary rule says that evidence gained as the result of an illegal act by police cannot be used in court. Use your print or online textbook to describe four circumstances under which "tainted evidence" is still admissible in court.

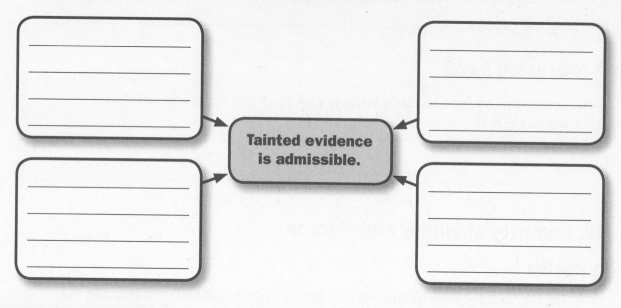

Tainted evidence is admissible.

What Do You Think?

D. What is the purpose of the exclusionary rule?

_____

_____

V. Rights of the Accused

Find Out

A. Review the rights of the accused in your print or online textbook. Then place each right into the appropriate part of the diagram below.

Rights of the Accused

At Arrest	Before Trial	During Trial	After Trial

CHAPTER 20 To what extent has the judiciary protected the rights of privacy, security, and personal freedom?

Name: _____

B. Review the case of *Miranda* v. *Arizona,* 1966, in your print or online textbook.

1. What did this case decide regarding self-incrimination?

_____

_____

2. When must the Miranda rights be read to a suspect?

_____

3. Write from memory four Miranda rights, below.

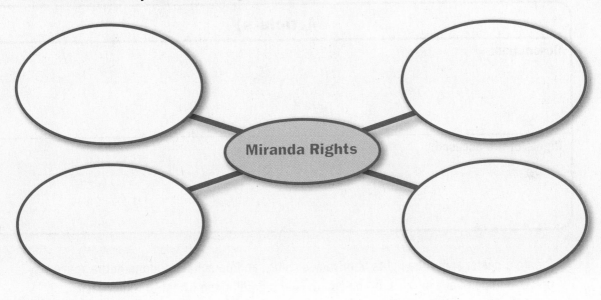

Miranda Rights

👤 What Do You Think?

C. Do you think the judiciary has extended <u>too many</u> protections or <u>not enough</u> protections for the rights of privacy, security, and personal freedom? Rate your opinion on the scale below, and then explain your answer.

Not Enough Protections								Too Many Protections

_____

_____

_____

_____

_____

_____

_____

_____

CHAPTER 20 To what extent has the judiciary protected the rights of privacy, security, and personal freedom?

Name: _____

Apply What You've Learned Activity

Scan print or online newspapers or news magazines for articles about criminal cases. Look for the inclusion of rights of the accused (bail, arraignment, the number of days before the trial is scheduled, defense attorney provided, and so on). In the space below, prepare a brief report describing the article(s) and the right(s) afforded to the accused.

Article(s)

Description:

Rights of the accused:

A. Create a poster about the rights of privacy, security, and personal freedom. In the space below, outline what you will show on your poster regarding the extent to which each freedom is protected.

I. Right of privacy

  A. _____

  B. _____

II. Right of security

  A. Home

    1. _____

    2. _____

  B. Person

    1. _____

    2. _____

  C. Vehicle

    1. _____

    2. _____

III. Right of personal freedom

  A. _____

  B. _____

CHAPTER 20 To what extent has the judiciary protected the rights of privacy, security, and personal freedom?

Name: _____

Essay

To what extent has the judiciary protected the rights of privacy, security, and personal freedom?

Americans' rights to privacy, security, and personal freedom are protected from the Federal Government by the Bill of Rights. The 14th Amendment's Due Process Clause applies most of those same protections against State governments.

"My client would like to plead the Fifth Amendment, Your Honor, and any other Amendment that you feel might be appropriate."

> **The criminal goes free, if he must, but it is the law that sets him free. Nothing can destroy a government more quickly than its failure to observe its own laws . . . .**
>
> — *Supreme Court Justice Tom C. Clark,* Mapp *v.* Ohio

What Do You Think?

What is your opinion? Write a response to the Essential Question, **To what extent has the judiciary protected the rights of privacy, security, and personal freedom?** Consider your thoughts on the information above, the Guiding Questions in your textbook, and the activities you have completed in your Journal. See page 219 for a rubric on writing an Essential Question essay.

Don't Forget

Your answer to this question will help you think about the Unit 5 Essential Question: **What should be the role of the judicial branch?**

CHAPTER 21 Civil Rights: Equal Justice Under Law

Warmup

Why are there ongoing struggles for civil rights?

A. Discrimination once limited the civil rights of minorities in the United States. What are civil rights? Write four examples of civil rights in the web diagram below.

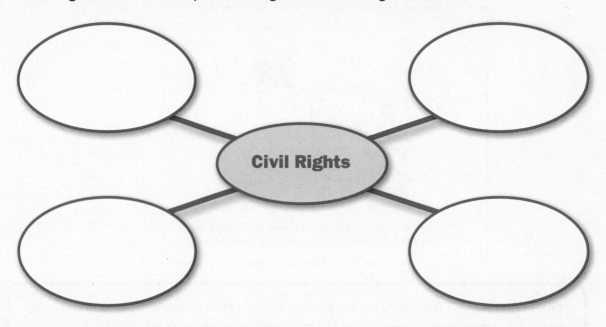

Civil Rights

B. On the scale below, where would you rate the level of the nation's civil rights coverage today? Explain your answer.

_____

_____

_____

_____

_____

_____

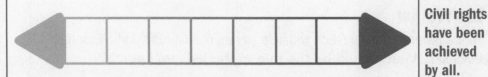

Civil rights are still denied to all minorities.

Civil rights have been achieved by all.

Exploration

I. Discrimination

➡ Find Out

A. The Declaration of Independence declares that "all men are created equal," and the 14th Amendment guarantees "equal protection of the laws" to all Americans. Still, discrimination of minorities was the norm until civil rights acts were passed in the 1950s. In the chart below, use information in your print or online textbook to show the effects of discrimination.

Cause	Effect(s) on Minority Group
1. *Plessy* v. *Ferguson,* 1896, legalizes race-based discrimination.	
2. Westward expansion leads to the forced relocation of Native Americans to reservations.	
3. White Americans resent Chinese contract laborers who work in mines and on railroads.	
4. Japan bombs Pearl Harbor, bringing the United States into World War II.	
5. Women are placed in a separate "sphere" of society by men.	

👤 What Do You Think?

B. In his "Letter From Birmingham Jail," civil rights leader Dr. Martin Luther King, Jr., wrote: "Oppressed people cannot remain oppressed forever. The yearning for freedom eventually manifests itself." In what ways did the struggle for civil rights manifest itself?

_____

_____

_____

_____

II. Challenging Segregation

⇨ Find Out

A. Use your print or online textbook to define or describe the following:

1. segregation: _____

_____

2. Jim Crow laws: _____

_____

3. separate-but-equal doctrine: _____

_____

4. integration: _____

_____

5. de jure segregation: _____

_____

6. de facto segregation: _____

_____

B. What important issue did each case decide regarding segregation in public schools?

1. *Missouri ex rel. Gaines* v. *Canada*, 1938

_____

_____

_____

2. *Brown* v. *Board of Education of Topeka*, 1954

_____

_____

_____

3. *Alexander* v. *Holmes County Board of Education*, 1969

_____

_____

_____

4. *Swann* v. *Charlotte-Mecklenburg Board of Education*, 1971

_____

_____

_____

C. In what other areas has legally-enforced racial segregation been eliminated? List four examples below.

_____　　_____

_____　　_____

D. List three examples of gender-based distinctions that the Supreme Court has found unconstitutional. Then list three examples that were upheld.

Gender-Based Distinctions	
Found Unconstitutional	**Found Constitutional**
Example:	Example:
Example:	Example:
Example:	Example:

E. On what two grounds will the Supreme Court uphold a law that treats women differently from men?

1. _____

_____

2. _____

_____

👤 What Do You Think?

F. Do you think women should have to register for the draft? Why or why not?

_____

_____

_____

_____

_____

III. Civil Rights Laws

➡ Find Out

A. Explain how the federal legislation below and on the next page guarantee the civil rights of African Americans, other minorities, and women.

> **1. Civil Rights Act of 1964**

> **2. Civil Rights Act of 1968**

> **3. Title IX**

B. What is affirmative action, and what is its purpose?

Definition: _____

_____

Purpose: _____

_____

👤 What Do You Think?

C. What does the passage of civil rights and voting rights laws suggest about how public attitudes about discrimination against African Americans have changed over time?

_____

_____

_____

Apply What You've Learned Activity

Research a civil rights leader in this country, including his or her ideals, struggles, and successes. Write your research notes on the worksheet below.

Civil Rights Leader: _____

Ideals:

Struggles:

Successes:

On another sheet of paper, create an annotated time line of civil rights legislation in this country from Reconstruction to today. Include brief descriptions of each law or act. In addition, include several quotes from famous civil rights leaders.

1868 States ratify the 14th Amendment, including the Equal Protection Clause.

Essay

 ## Why are there ongoing struggles for civil rights?

The civil rights movement led to profound legal and social changes for American minorities. Today, de jure segregation is prohibited in the United States, but de facto segregation still exists in some schools and housing.

'Today we'll learn about segregation in America.'

> " We know through painful experience that freedom is never voluntarily given by the oppressor; it must be demanded by the oppressed. . . . For years now I have heard the word 'Wait!' It rings in the ear of every Negro with piercing familiarity. This 'Wait' has almost always meant 'Never.' We must come to see, with one of our distinguished jurists, that 'justice too long delayed is justice denied.'
>
> — *Dr. Martin Luther King, Jr.,* "Letter From Birmingham Jail," *1963*

What Do You Think?

What is your opinion? Write a response to the Essential Question, **How can the judiciary balance individual rights with the common good?** Consider your thoughts on the information above, the Guiding Questions in your textbook, and the activities you have completed in your Journal. See page 219 for a rubric on writing an Essential Question essay.

Don't Forget
Your answer to this question will help you think about the Unit 5 Essential Question: **What should be the role of the judicial branch?**

UNIT 5 The Judicial Branch

Essay Warmup

Examine the following perspectives on the judicial branch. The questions that follow the perspectives will help you focus your thinking on the Unit 5 Essential Question, **What should be the role of the judicial branch?**

> **Historically, the judicial branch has often been the sole protector of the rights of minority groups against the will of the popular majority.**
>
> — *Rep. Diane Watson (D., California)*

> **Laws are dead letters without courts to expound and define their true meaning and operation.**
>
> — *Alexander Hamilton,* The Federalist *No. 78*

1. What do Watson and Hamilton think the role of the judicial branch should be?

_____

_____

_____

_____

_____

> **We want courts to settle the question of whether someone has exceeded the limits set by the law. And we want judges to be free of essential dependence upon the wielders of power so that they can do what they are supposed to do without being intimidated.**
>
> — *Joseph Tussman,* Judicial Activism and the Rule of Law: Toward a Theory of Selective Intervention

2. Why does Tussman believe judges need to act independently?

_____

_____

_____

_____

_____

UNIT 5 The Judicial Branch

Frank and Ernest

IT'S EITHER CONSTITUTIONAL OR UNCONSTITUTIONAL--- WE <u>DON'T</u> USE A SCALE OF ONE TO TEN!

©2006 Thaves. www.cartoonistgroup.com

THAVES

3. What is the cartoonist saying about the role of the judicial branch?

_____

_____

_____

4. How do 5–4 split decisions by the Supreme Court, as well as precedents overturned by later Court decisions, contradict this cartoonist's message?

_____

_____

_____

👤 What Do You Think?

5. Choose one of the documents above and explain how it helps you answer the Unit 5 Essential Question, **What should be the role of the judicial branch?**

_____

_____

_____

_____

_____

_____

_____

UNIT 5 The Judicial Branch

Essay

 What should be the role of the judicial branch?

Write an essay that answers the Essential Question, **What should be the role of the judicial branch?** Use your answers to the Essential Question warmup questions on the previous pages, your answers to the chapter Essential Questions, and what you have learned in this unit. Keep in mind that your essay should reflect your thoughtful and well-supported personal point of view. Answering the prompts below will help you structure your essay. Go to page 219 for a rubric for writing an Essential Question essay.

Thesis Statement: _____

_____

Body Paragraph 1	Body Paragraph 2	Body Paragraph 3
Main Idea	**Main Idea**	**Main Idea**
_____ _____ _____ _____	_____ _____ _____ _____	_____ _____ _____ _____
Supporting Details	**Supporting Details**	**Supporting Details**
1. _____ _____ _____	1. _____ _____ _____	1. _____ _____ _____
2. _____ _____ _____	2. _____ _____ _____	2. _____ _____ _____
3. _____ _____ _____	3. _____ _____ _____	3. _____ _____ _____

Conclusion: _____

_____

Comparative Political and Economic Systems

 Essential Question

How should a government meet the needs of its people?

Chapter 22 Essential Question

How should you measure different governments?

Chapter 23 Essential Question

To what extent should governments participate in the economy?

UNIT 6 Comparative Political and Economic Systems

Warmup

How should a government meet the needs of its people?

Throughout history societies have developed various forms of government—from absolute monarchies ruled by god-kings to modern representative democracies, such as the United States. Each system has ruled its people differently. Some have been authoritarian and repressive. Others have been based, to a greater or lesser extent, on the rule of the people. What should the relationship be between a government and its people? In Unit 6, you will learn about forms of government from ancient times to today and explore possible responses to the Essential Question above.

The Framers of the U.S. Constitution drew many of their ideas about government from the Roman Republic.

A. List ten responsibilities or duties that you think any government should fulfill.

_____ _____

_____ _____

_____ _____

_____ _____

_____ _____

B. Consider what you have learned about government in the United States. In your opinion, how well does government in this nation meet the needs of its people? Include examples to support your opinion.

_____

_____

_____

_____

_____

_____

CHAPTER 22

Comparative Political Systems

Warmup

 ## How should you measure different governments?

A. What do you think makes a government good or bad, successful or unsuccessful? List five characteristics of a good government and five of a bad governmet.

Characteristics of Good and Bad Governments	
Good	Bad

B. Where would you place the U.S. government on a scale of good government?

Best | | | | | | | | | | Worst

C. Explain your answer.

_____

_____

_____

_____

_____

_____

Exploration

I. Early Governments

→ Find Out

A. Using your print or online textbook or other resources, complete the chart by listing structures and features of Athenian democracy and the Roman Republic.

Feature	Athenian Democracy	Roman Republic
General Structure	direct democracy in which all citizens could participate	
Legislative Body/Bodies		
Executive		
Judicial Body		
Requirements for Citizenship		
Form of Law		

B. What legitimacy did the governments of Athens and Rome have for their rule?

_____

_____

_____

👤 What Do You Think?

C. Based on the information in your chart, under which system would you have the most rights and freedoms? Explain.

_____

_____

II. Fascist and Communist Governments

→ Find Out

A. Using your online or print textbook, complete the Venn diagram to compare and contrast features of fascist and Communist governments.

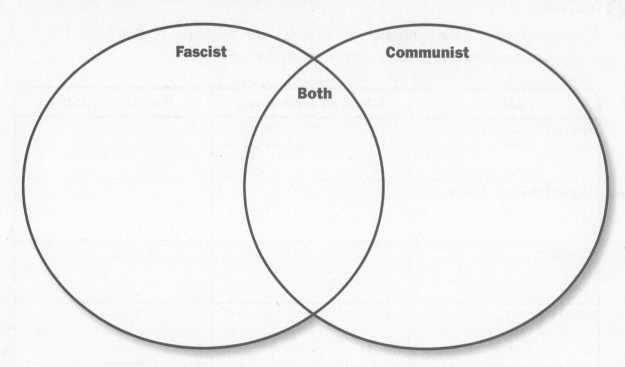

Fascist   Both   Communist

B. Especially since the Enlightenment, the belief has grown that political power starts with the people, who give their leaders consent to rule. This principle is called popular sovereignty. How do fascist and Communist governments use the idea of popular sovereignty to legitimize their rule?

_____

_____

_____

● What Do You Think?

C. Review your characteristics of a good or a bad government in the Chapter 22 Warmup. Based on those characteristics, where do you think Nazi Germany and Communist U.S.S.R. would appear on the scale of best/worst government? Explain.

_____

_____

_____

_____

III. Popular Sovereignty and Democratization

→ Find Out

A. Popular sovereignty is a necessary ingredient in building a democracy, or
democratization. Using your textbook and other print or Internet sources, find out
about the level of popular sovereignty and democratization in each nation below.
Then grade each from 1 to 5, with 5 being failure, on its level of democratization.
Explain your reasons for that grade, including other ingredients for a successful
democracy that each nation may have or may lack.

Nation	Grade	Reasons for Grade
Mexico		
Russia		
Haiti		
Afghanistan		
United States	1	The United States is a democracy, based on popular sovereignty, with a free press, multiple parties, a civilian controlled military, equal economic opportunity, a professional civil service, and a lot of common trust among citizens.
United Kingdom		
Iraq		

👤 What Do You Think?

B. To which nation did you give the lowest grade? Give two ways in which you think this
nation could increase popular sovereignty and make the transition to democracy.

_____

_____

Apply What You've Learned Activity

How well do different governments work today? Use this worksheet to answer the Apply What You've Learned questions in your print or online textbook. Interview an immigrant you may know about the government in his or her native country. Use the table below to summarize the responses you receive in preparation for completing the Essential Question Assessment.

Why did you come to the United States?	
How do you view the government of your native country?	
What do you think worked well?	
How well did your government meet citizens' needs?	
How democratic do you think it is?	
How do you view the government of the United States in comparison to that of your native country?	

A. Choose three nations from three different continents—for example, China, France, and Chile. You may want to include your interviewee's nation, as well. On a separate sheet of paper, make a chart with a column for each country, and for the United States. Use your chart to record basic information about the structure and function of the U.S. government compared to each of the other countries in the chart.

B. Use the information in your chart to create your comparative national government guide as directed in the Essential Question Assessment.

Essay

How should you measure different governments?

In the last 200 years, there has been an extension of popular sovereignty around the world. However, societies still approach government differently or are faced with specialized challenges, and democratization has not taken place everywhere. Consider the quotations about government, below.

> **The power . . . to cast a man into prison without formulating any charge known to the law, and particularly to deny him the judgment of his peers, is in the highest degree odious [horrible] and is the foundation of all totalitarian government whether Nazi or Communist.**
>
> — *British Prime Minister Winston Churchill*

> **The only sure bulwark [defense] of continuing liberty is a government strong enough to protect the interests of the people, and a people strong enough and well enough informed to maintain its sovereign control over the government.**
>
> — *President Franklin Delano Roosevelt*

What Do You Think?

What is your opinion? Write a response to the Essential Question, **How should you measure different governments?** Consider your thoughts on the quotations above, the Guiding Questions in your textbook, and the activities you have completed in your Journal. See page 219 for a rubric for writing an Essential Question essay.

 Don't Forget

Your answer to this question will help you think about the Unit 6 Essential Question: **How should a government meet the needs of its people?**

CHAPTER 23 Comparative Economic Systems

Warmup

 To what extent should governments participate in the economy?

A. Think about the economic choices you make each day. How do your choices demonstrate your economic freedom? Complete the concept web with words and phrases that that you think relate to or describe economic freedom.

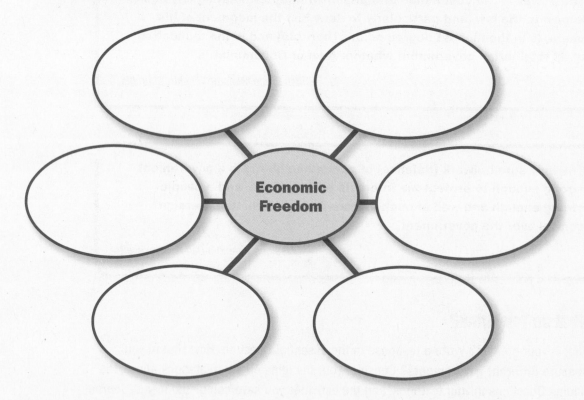

Economic Freedom

B. Think about the participation of the government in the economy. This includes taxes, labor laws, and regulations on goods and services. Describe one way in which you are limited by the government's participation in the economy and one way in which you benefit from it. Give reasons to support your choices.

_____

_____

_____

_____

CHAPTER 23 To what extent should governments participate in
the economy?

Name: _____

Exploration

I. Capitalism

➔ Find Out

A. Use your print or online textbook to provide descriptions and examples for each feature
of the capitalist free enterprise system in the United States.

Feature of Free Enterprise System	Description	Example
Private Ownership		
Individual Initiative		
Profit	benefits from investment or business; pushes entrepreneurs to take risks	If a company does well, investors make a profit in the form of a dividend.
Competition		

👤 What Do You Think?

B. What is the *laissez-faire theory?* Is the U.S. government's approach to the economy
laissez-faire? Why or why not?

_____

_____

_____

C. What do you think the economy would be like if markets were totally free and the
government was completely laissez-faire? Explain.

_____

_____

_____

CHAPTER 23 To what extent should governments participate in the economy?

Name: _____

II. Socialism and Communism

→ Find Out

A. Socialist and Communist governments were established, in theory, to do a better job at meeting their people's needs than capitalist nations did. Based on information in your print or online textbook, summarize what needs each system was trying to meet and the methods it used.

■ Goals of socialist governments:

_____

_____

_____

■ Methods of socialist governments:

_____

_____

_____

_____

■ Goals of Communist governments:

_____

_____

_____

■ Methods of Communist governments:

_____

_____

_____

● What Do You Think?

B. Although some socialist governments have been relatively successful, Communist governments, with the exception of a very few, have not been able to stay in power. Why do you think that is?

_____

_____

_____

_____

_____

CHAPTER 23 To what extent should governments participate in the economy?

Name: _____

III. The U.S. Government and the Economy

➡ Find Out

A. List five ways in which the U.S. government participates in the domestic economy and five ways in which it does so in the global economy.

U.S. Government/Domestic Economy	U.S. Government/Global Economy
The SEC oversees the stock market and prevents stock trade abuses and crimes.	It belongs to the World Trade Organization, to help increase world trade.

B. What is *globalization*? Write a definition in your own words. Then explain how globalization affects the United States.

_____

_____

_____

👤 What Do You Think?

C. Choose one item from each column in the chart above. What do you think the impact would be on the U.S. economy and society if the government stopped performing these tasks or responsibilities?

_____

_____

_____

_____

_____

Apply What You've Learned Activity

Ideas about how much involvement the government should have in the economy have been discussed for hundreds of years. Today, people still debate the issue. Interview a business owner in your community to find out what he or she thinks. Use the table below to summarize the responses you receive in preparation for completing the Essential Question Assessment.

How do you think the American system of government supports or encourages economic freedom?	
How does a free market help your business?	
How do you think your life or your business would be different in a socialist or Communist system?	
Do you think that the Federal Government should be more or less involved in the economy, workers' rights, and social welfare?	

A. Which opinions do you agree or disagree with most? Explain.

_____

_____

B. In preparation for writing your political statement for the Essential Question Assessment, write a thesis sentence that summarizes this business owner's opinions on the role of government in the economy.

_____

_____

CHAPTER 23 To what extent should governments participate in the economy?

Name: _____

Essay

To what extent should governments participate in the economy?

How much should the government participate in the economy? Is government participation necessary or should the United States have as close to a free market economy as possible? Consider the views on government and the economy, below.

> When a government takes over a people's economic life it becomes absolute, and when it has become absolute it destroys the arts, the minds, the liberties and the meaning of the people it governs.
>
> — *Maxwell Anderson,* The Guaranteed Life

> If the people cannot trust their government to do the job for which it exists—to protect them and to promote their common welfare— all else is lost.
>
> — *President Barack Obama*

What Do You Think?

What is your opinion? Write a response to the Essential Question, **To what extent should governments participate in the economy?** Consider your thoughts on the quotations above, the Guiding Questions in your textbook, and the activities you have completed in your Journal. See page 219 for a rubric for writing an Essential Question essay.

Don't Forget

Your answer to this question will help you think about the Unit 6 Essential Question: **How should a government meet the needs of its people?**

UNIT 6 Comparative Political and Economic Systems

Essay Warmup

Examine the following perspectives on government and the people. The questions that follow each perspective will help focus your thinking on the Unit 6 Essential Question, **How should a government meet the needs of its people?**

> **ON THE LIMITS OF GOVERNMENT:**
> Conservatives know that governments don't have all the answers. But if they govern with the right values, they can make a real difference.
>
> — *U.K. Conservative Party Manifesto, 2005*

1. What do you think the U.K. Conservative Party means when it says, "Conservatives know that governments don't have all the answers"?

_____

_____

2. Do you agree or disagree that government leaders should apply their "values" to how they govern? Explain.

_____

_____

> **ON THE RESPONSIBILITIES OF A COMMUNIST PARTY:**
> Without the efforts of the Chinese Communist Party, without the Chinese Communists as the mainstay of the Chinese people, China can never achieve independence and liberation, or industrialization and the modernization of her agriculture.
>
> — *Mao Zedong, 1945*

3. What did Mao see as the main duties of his party and government?

_____

_____

Prosperity Indicators, U.S.

	1950	2007
Life Expectancy at Birth (years)	68.2	78.0
Per Capita Gross Domestic Product (constant 2000 dollars)	$11,720*	$38,020
Population with Bachelor's Degrees, age 25 and up	6.2%	28.7%

*approximate

By most measures, Americans are healthier, better educated, and more affluent today than in the past.

4. Study the data above and answer the following questions:

a. Which item in the chart do you think shows the most significant improvement between 1950 and 2007?

_____

b. Based on this data, what, if any, connection do you think there is between education and per capita GDP?

_____

_____

c. Do you think that these three measurements could have been based on government participation in the economy? Why or why not?

_____

_____

_____

👤 What Do You Think?

5. Choose one of the following documents above and explain how it helps you answer the Unit 6 Essential Question, **How should a government meet the needs of its people?**

_____

_____

_____

_____

_____

_____

UNIT 6 Comparative Political and Economic Systems

Essay

 How should a government meet the needs of its people?

Write an essay that responds to the Unit 6 Essential Question, **How should a government meet the needs of its people?** Use your answers to the Essential Question warmups on the previous pages, your answers to the chapter Essential Questions, and what you have learned in this unit. Keep in mind that your essay should reflect your thoughtful and well-supported personal point of view. Filling in the chart below will help you structure your essay. Go to page 219 for a rubric for writing an Essential Question essay.

Thesis Statement: _____
_____

Body Paragraph 1	Body Paragraph 2	Body Paragraph 3
Main Idea _____ _____ _____ _____	**Main Idea** _____ _____ _____ _____	**Main Idea** _____ _____ _____ _____
Supporting Details 1. _____ _____ 2. _____ _____ 3. _____ _____	**Supporting Details** 1. _____ _____ 2. _____ _____ 3. _____ _____	**Supporting Details** 1. _____ _____ 2. _____ _____ 3. _____ _____

Conclusion: _____
_____

Unit 7

Participating in State and Local Government

 Essential Question

What is the right balance of local, State, and federal government?

Chapter 24 Essential Question

How much power should State government have?

Chapter 25 Essential Question

How local should government be?

UNIT 7 Participating in State and Local Government

Warmup

What is the right balance of local, State, and federal government?

Some Americans favor a strong National Government, while others feel that State and local governments should have the most power. How do you think power should be shared? In Unit 7, you will learn about the structure and functions of State and local governments and explore possible responses to the Essential Question above.

The Federal Government shares the cost of highway projects like Boston's Big Dig with the States and counties where they are built.

A. List the name of each level of government under which you live. In the last column, number the levels of government from 1 to 5 based on how much each level affects your daily life. (If you live in a State with no counties or special districts, then number the levels accordingly.)

National	United States	
State		
County/Parish/Borough		
Special District		
Community		

B. For each power or responsibility of government, write *F* on the line if you think it should be the responsibility of the U.S. Federal Government, *S* if you think it should be under the State government, or *L* if you think it should be carried out by local government. If you think levels should share responsibility, write more than one letter.

___ income taxes

___ disaster management

___ drivers' licenses

___ international diplomacy

___ environmental protection

___ national defense

___ elementary and high schools

___ welfare and unemployment payments

___ police and fire protection

___ highway and bridge maintenance

24 Governing the States

Warmup

 ## How much power should State government have?

A. The Tenth Amendment describes the division of powers between the Federal Government and the States.

> **The powers not delegated to the United States by the Constitution, nor prohibited by it to the States, are reserved to the States respectively, or to the people.**
>
> — *Tenth Amendment to the U.S. Constitution*

In your own words, explain the meaning of this amendment and why you think the Framers added it to the Constitution.

_____

_____

_____

_____

_____

B. Think about State and local government in your State. What do you think it would be like if there was no State government—just national and local governments? What would it be like if there was only a State government and no federal or local governments? Would citizens' needs still be met in either case? Explain, using specific examples to support your opinions.

_____

_____

_____

_____

_____

_____

_____

Exploration

I. State Constitutions

→ **Find Out**

A. Like the U.S. Constitution, all State constitutions include a bill of rights based on popular sovereignty and limited government. The writers of these documents wanted to ensure that the government was under the control of the citizens, and not the reverse. Study a copy of your State's constitution. In the chart below list at least ten provisions that limit the power of the State and protect popular sovereignty.

My State's Constitution
1.
2.
3.
4.
5.
6.
7.
8.
9.
10.

B. How is the constitution amended in your State? Describe the process(es) here.

_____

_____

👤 **What Do You Think?**

C. How well do you think your State's constitution and amendment processes limit the State's power and protect your rights as a citizen?

_____

_____

II. State Legislature

➔ Find Out

A. A State legislature has all powers that (1) the State constitution does not grant exclusively to the executive or judicial branches or to local governments and (2) that neither the State constitution nor the U.S. Constitution denies to it. Using your print or online textbook and your State's constitution, fill in the chart by listing some of the main powers of your State's legislature.

Powers of the State Legislature	
Lawmaking Powers	**Non-lawmaking Powers**

B. What is the *police power?* Give at least three examples of how State legislatures use this power.

_____

_____

👤 What Do You Think?

C. Why do you think that the police power is considered the most important power of State legislatures? Why do you think the Framers of the U.S. Constitution reserved this power to the States and not to the National Government?

_____

_____

_____

_____

III. Powers of the State Governor

→ Find Out

A. Using your print or online textbook, your State's constitution, and your knowledge of government, complete the concept web to list the powers of your State's governor.

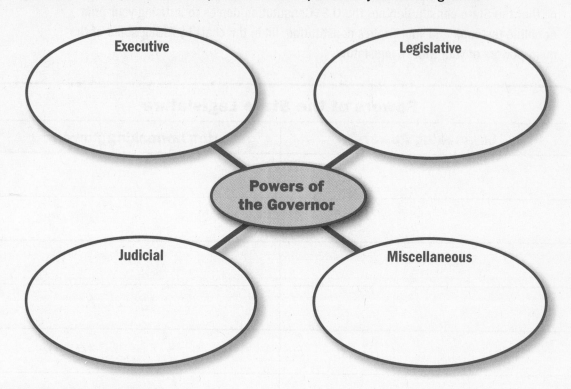

👤 What Do You Think?

B. Of the powers you recorded above, which three do you think are the most important to a State governor? Why?

Power 1: _____

_____

_____

Power 2: _____

_____

_____

Power 3: _____

_____

_____

IV. Courts and the Law

→ Find Out

A. Using your print or online textbook and your knowledge of government, complete the flowchart to show the levels of courts in the United States from local courts to the U.S. Supreme Court. Then describe the main jurisdiction or duties of each level. (There may be more or fewer steps, depending on your community and State.)

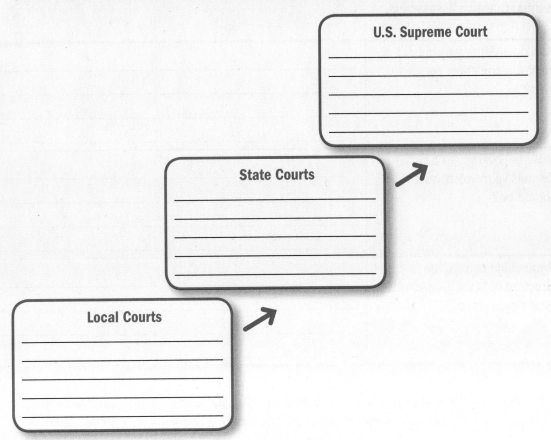

U.S. Supreme Court
_____
_____
_____
_____

State Courts
_____
_____
_____
_____

Local Courts
_____
_____
_____
_____

B. Read Article VI, Clause 2 of the U.S. Constitution—the Supremacy Clause. Then write a summary of the clause in your own words below.

_____
_____

👤 What Do You Think?

C. Why do you think that State law is always subordinate to federal law? What would happen if the States could make laws that contradicted the U.S. Constitution?

_____
_____
_____

Apply What You've Learned Activity

What do members of your State government think about its effectiveness? Use this worksheet to answer the Apply What You've Learned questions in your print or online textbook. Interview a legislator, legislative aid, or member of the State government. Use the table below to summarize the responses you receive in preparation for completing the Essential Question Assessment.

How does State government most directly affect people's lives?	_____ _____ _____ _____
Is State government as responsive to voters as it should be?	_____ _____ _____ _____
If you could change the structure of State government what would you do?	_____ _____ _____ _____

A. Based on the answers to your interview questions, what you learned from this chapter, and your prior knowledge, list some changes to government that you think need to be made.

_____

_____

_____

_____

B. Select one of the changes from your list above, and then write a statement that describes the purpose and goals of your proposed amendment.

_____

_____

_____

_____

Essay

 ## How much power should State government have?

What the balance of power should be between the Federal Government and the States has been debated since before the U.S. Constitution existed. This issue was a major concern to the Framers; later, arguments about State versus Federal power led to civil war. The debate continues today. Consider the historic and modern views on this issue, below.

> The constitution should be so formed as not to swallow up the state governments: the general government ought to be confined to certain national object[ive]s; and the states should retain such powers, as concern their own internal [welfare]."
>
> — *Delegate at the New York State Constitutional Convention, 1789*

> Only a few years ago, the Supreme Court appeared to be on the verge of gravely altering the balance of power between the federal government and the states . . . . if taken too far, the reinvigoration of state-level power threatened to encumber the federal government in such critical areas as civil rights and environmental protection."
>
> — *Excerpt from "States' Rights Revision,"* The Washington Post, *July 13, 2004*

What Do You Think?

What is your opinion? Write a response to the Essential Question, **How much power should State government have?** Consider your thoughts on the quotations above, the Guiding Questions in your textbook, and the activities you have completed in your Journal. See page 219 for a rubric for writing an Essential Question essay.

 ### Don't Forget

Your answer to this question will help you think about the Unit 7 Essential Question: **What is the right balance of local, State, and federal government?**

CHAPTER 25 Local Government and Finance

Warmup

How local should government be?

A. Complete the chart below by listing three government programs, responsibilities, or duties that you think should be carried out at each level of government in each category. Some examples have been provided.

	Local	**State**	**Federal**
Only	1. fire protection	1. sales taxes	1. national defence
	2.	2.	2.
	3.	3.	3.
Never	1. national defense	1. national defense	1.
	2.	2.	2.
	3.	3.	3.
Shared	1. welfare	1. welfare	1. welfare
	2.	2.	2.
	3.	3.	3.

B. Explain why you listed the items you did in the "Only" category for local government.

_____

_____

_____

Exploration

I. Local Government

⮕ Find Out

A. Use your online or print textbook, your town records or annual reports, community Web sites, and other resources to answer these questions about your local government:

Name of community: _____ Date of incorporation: _____

Is your community urban, rural, or suburban? _____

Describe the form and structure of your community's government. For example, is the community led by a mayor, a manager, or a board of selectpersons? What are the terms of these officials? Does your community have town meetings? How often are community elections?

_____

_____

_____

Name five main departments in your local government and an example of the service(s) each provides: _____

_____

_____

_____

_____

👤 What Do You Think?

B. Rank the departments and services you listed above in order according to how much each affects you personally. Explain the reasons for the order you chose.

- ■ _____
- ■ _____
- ■ _____
- ■ _____
- ■ _____

C. What individual or group has the most power or authority in your community government? Explain your thinking.

_____

_____

State and Local Spending

Find Out

A. State and local governments spend billions of dollars a year to provide services. Use print or Internet resources, such as State or the U.S. Census Bureau Web sites, to record data and create a circle graph that shows State and local spending in your State for the following categories:

Education: $ _____   Healthcare: $ _____

Public welfare: $ _____   Utilities: $ _____

Public safety: $ _____   Other: $ _____

Transportation: $ _____

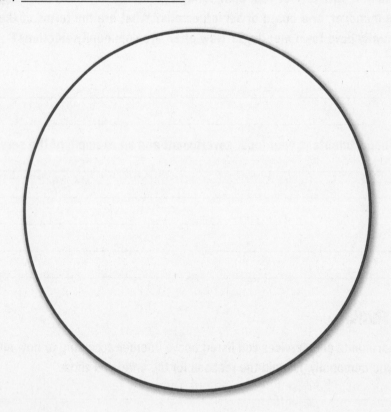

What Do You Think?

B. Which of the services in the circle graph do you receive? Circle them. Choose one of the circled services and explain why you think it is best provided by the State, local, or federal governments.

_____

_____

_____

_____

III. State and Local Revenues

➔ Find Out

A. List two taxes or fees that are levied by your local and by your State governments. Then, using Adam Smith's four criteria for a "good" tax from your online or print textbook, determine if these revenue sources qualify as "good" taxes. Circle yes or no.

Local Tax / Fee 1	
☐ equal ☐ certain ☐ convenient ☐ economical	= "good" tax; Yes or No
Local Tax / Fee 2	
☐ equal ☐ certain ☐ convenient ☐ economical	= "good" tax; Yes or No
State Tax / Fee 1	
☐ equal ☐ certain ☐ convenient ☐ economical	= "good" tax; Yes or No
State Tax / Fee 2	
☐ equal ☐ certain ☐ convenient ☐ economical	= "good" tax; Yes or No

👤 What Do You Think?

B. Some States do not levy an income tax. Often in these States, property taxes make up revenues that would be raised by income taxes. Property taxes are levied by local governments, but in States without income tax, property taxes are often relatively high. Which do you think is fairer—a State income tax that all State residents pay based on their incomes or local property taxes that might vary considerably from community to community, and are paid only by property owners? Explain.

_____

_____

_____

_____

Apply What You've Learned Activity

What have you learned about the structure and budgets of your community or county? Use this worksheet to answer the Apply What You've Learned questions and to prepare to complete the Essential Question Assessment.

A. Which positions at the community or county level are elected and which are appointed?

Elected	Appointed

B. What are the most costly programs at the community or county level?

_____

_____

C. Which officials have the greatest authority over the budget?

_____

D. What responsibilities does the State require of the community or county government?

_____

_____

_____

E. For the Essential Question Assessment you will create a brochure for a fictional candidate to one of the community or county offices. Select one of the officials from the table in Part A to be the focus of your brochure: _____.

Essay

 How local should government be?

What is the role of local government today? What responsibilities do you think should belong at the local, State, or federal levels? Consider the views on the levels of government, below.

> " The Federal Government should be the last resort, not the first. Ask if a potential program is truly a federal responsibility or whether it can better be handled . . . by local or state governments."
>
> — *Donald Rumsfeld, U.S. Secretary of Defense*

> " Encroachments of the States on the general authority, sacrifices of national to local interests, [and] interferences of the measures of different States, form a great part of the history of our political system."
>
> — *James Madison, explaining the need for a strong National Government*

What Do You Think?

What is your opinion? Write a response to the Essential Question, **How local should government be?** Consider your thoughts on the quotations above, the Guiding Questions in your textbook, and the activities you have completed in your Journal. See page 219 for a rubric for writing an Essential Question essay.

 Don't Forget

Your answer to this question will help you think about the Unit 7 Essential Question: **What is the right balance of local, State, and federal government?**

UNIT 7 Participating in State and Local Government

Essay Warmup

Examine the following perspectives on State and local government. The questions that follow each perspective will help you focus your thinking on the Unit 7 Essential Question, **What is the right balance of local, State, and federal government?**

> **ON THE ROLE OF THE FEDERAL GOVERNMENT:**
>
> **It is my intention to curb the size and influence of the Federal establishment and to demand recognition of the distinction between the powers granted to the Federal Government and those reserved to the States or to the people. All of us need to be reminded that the Federal Government did not create the States; the States created the Federal Government.**
>
> — *Ronald Reagan, First Inaugural Speech, 1981*

1. Why does Reagan say he wants to "curb the size and influence" of the Federal Government?

_____

_____

2. Do you agree with his assessment? Why or why not?

_____

_____

> **ON THE VALUE OF MAYORS:**
>
> **As CEO's of the nation's cities, mayors know all too well the challenges American families face daily, so we are in the best position to offer solutions to local problems.**
>
> — *Mayor Douglas Palmer, Trenton, New Jersey (then President of the U.S. Conference of Mayors)*

3. Do you agree that mayors are always in the best position to deal with local problems? What role do State leaders play that mayors cannot?

_____

_____

Name: _____

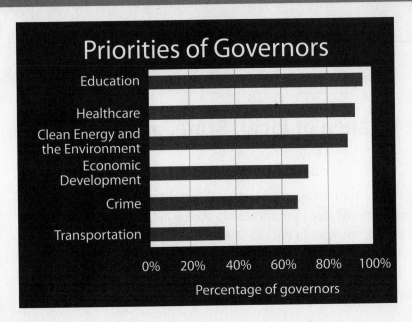

Priorities of Governors

Education
Healthcare
Clean Energy and the Environment
Economic Development
Crime
Transportation

0%   20%   40%   60%   80%   100%

Percentage of governors

Each year, the National Association of Governors tracks the governors' State of the State addresses and identifies the subjects mentioned by the most governors in their speeches.

4. Study the bar graph and answer the following questions:

a. List the priorities in order from highest to lowest based on governors' State of the State addresses.

_____

_____

b. Why do you think these are priorities for governors? Do you think they would be for the President or for a city mayor?

_____

_____

c. Do you agree with the order of these priorities? Why or why not?

_____

_____

_____

👤 What Do You Think?

5. Choose one of the following documents above and explain how it helps you answer the Unit 7 Essential Question, **What is the right balance of local, State, and federal government?**

_____

_____

_____

Essay

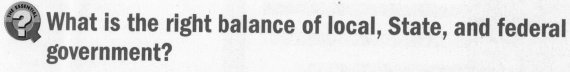

What is the right balance of local, State, and federal government?

Write an essay that responds to the Unit 7 Essential Question, **What is the right balance of local, State, and federal government?** Use your answers to the Essential Question warmups on the previous pages, your answers to the chapter Essential Questions, and what you have learned in this unit. Keep in mind that your essay should reflect your thoughtful and well-supported personal point of view. Filling in the chart below will help you structure your essay. Go to page 219 for a rubric for writing an Essential Question essay.

Thesis Statement: _____

_____

Body Paragraph 1	Body Paragraph 2	Body Paragraph 3
Main Idea	**Main Idea**	**Main Idea**
_____	_____	_____
_____	_____	_____
_____	_____	_____
_____	_____	_____
Supporting Details	**Supporting Details**	**Supporting Details**
1. _____	1. _____	1. _____
_____	_____	_____
_____	_____	_____
2. _____	2. _____	2. _____
_____	_____	_____
_____	_____	_____
3. _____	3. _____	3. _____
_____	_____	_____

Conclusion: _____

_____

Rubric for Essential Question Essays

Criteria	Exceeds standard	Meets standard	Approaches standard	Does not meet standard
Thesis	Clear, well-developed thesis with clear connection to Essential Question	Clear and mostly developed thesis with clear connection to Essential Question	Somewhat clear thesis with limited connection to Essential Question	Unclear, or clear with little connection to Essential Question
Introduction	Clear, direct focus, highly interesting and engaging, provides excellent context for discussing Essential Question.	Focused and interesting, provides context for discussing Essential Question.	Somewhat focused and interesting, provides some limited context for discussing Essential Question.	Too broad, provides little context for discussing Essential Question. Uses throwaway phrases like "throughout history."
Supporting evidence and facts	Substantial facts and evidence	Sufficient facts and evidence	Uneven use of facts and evidence	Insufficient facts and evidence
Analysis	Effective, logical, sophisticated analysis; facts and evidence substantially enhance analysis; demonstrates keen insight into and understanding of Essential Question.	Effective, logical analysis; facts and evidence enhance analysis; demonstrates clear understanding of Essential Question.	General analysis only, and/or somewhat illogical or inconsistent. Facts and evidence somewhat enhance analysis; demonstrates basic understanding of Essential Question.	Limited analysis and/or illogical. Uses descriptive and storytelling format rather than analysis; demonstrates limited understanding of Essential Question.
Conclusion	Ties together main ideas to arrive at a logical and insightful conclusion that shows deep understanding of the Essential Question.	Ties together main ideas to arrive at a logical and insightful conclusion.	Demonstrates some understanding of the Essential Question and/or relies heavily on summary.	Demonstrates general and shallow understanding of the Essential Question or is summary only.
Organization and mechanics	Highly effective writing and organization; makes extremely few or no grammatical errors.	Effective writing and organization; makes few grammatical errors, which do not distract from the overall quality of the paper	Acceptable writing and organization. Some errors in spelling, grammar, punctuation, word choice, and capitalization. Includes repetition, fragments, conversational prose.	Weak organization and/or writing skills; many errors which detract from the quality of the paper

Photo and Art Credits

Every effort has been made to secure permission and provide appropriate credit for photographic material. The publisher deeply regrets any omission and pledges to correct errors called to its attention in subsequent editions.

Unless otherwise acknowledged, all photographs are the property of Pearson Education, Inc.

Notes

Notes